1740 River Don Navigation Act

1741

1742 Benjamin Huntsman's discovery of cast steel.

1743 Thomas Bolsover produced Sheffield Plate.

1744

1745 *Jacobite Rising under Bonnie Prince Charlie.*

1746 Walker Bros. built the first foundry at Masborough.

1747

1748 *End of the War of the Austrian Succession.*

1749

1750

1751

1752 First Elsecar Colliery opened.

1753

1754

1755

1756 *Opening of Seven Years War.*

1757

1758

1759

1760 *Accession of George III*

1761 Bridgewater Canal opened.

1762

1763 *Peace of Paris.*

1764 Hargreaves invents the Spinning Jenny.

1765

1766

1767 Iron rails made at Coalbrookdale. First coke furnace at Masborough

1768

1769 Watt patents his first steam engine. Arkwright patents the Water Frame

1770

1771 First water-powered cotton spinning mill at Cromford.

1772 Cockshutt's patent for producing malleable iron at Wortley.

1773 Chesterfield to Gainsborough canal built.

1774

1775 *War of American Independence*

1776 Crompton invents the Mule. First mill at Belper.

1777 Grand Trunk Canal opened.

1778

1779

THEN AND THERE SERIES
GENERAL EDITOR
MARJORIE REEVES, M.A., PH.D.

A Textile Community in the Industrial Revolution

E. G. POWER

Illustrated from contemporary sources

LONGMANS

LONGMANS, GREEN AND CO LTD
London and Harlow
Associated companies, branches and representatives throughout the world

© Longmans, Green & Co. Ltd. 1969
First published 1969
Second impression 1969

SBN 582 20420 8

Printed in Malta by
St Paul's Press Ltd

ACKNOWLEDGEMENTS

We are grateful to Mrs. Agnes H. Kay for permission to quote from the *Harrison Papers*.

Photographs were reproduced by permission of the following: Ariel Press p. 50; British Museum pp. 6, 7, 11, 13, 16, 20, 30, 32, 33, 36, 45, 55, 61, 64, 66, 69, 71, 74, 75, 80, 84, 85, 87, 88, 102, 104; Connoisseur Publishing Co. p. 67. The Syndics of the Fitzwilliam Museum, Cambridge p. 18; Helmshore Local History Society p. 78; Nottingham Castle Art Gallery p. 49; the Earl of Mansfield p. 96; J. M. Richards, *The Functional Tradition in Early Industrial Buildings*, The Architectural Press (photographer John Piper) p. 39; A. N. Smith Esq. pp. 5, 22, 24, 25, 42; Victoria & Albert Museum Crown Copyright pp. 47, 93.

The drawing on p. 53 was reproduced by permission of William Hollins & Co. Ltd., Nottingham and that on p. 43 by Kenneth Hudson, *An Introduction to Industrial Archaeology*, John Baker Ltd.

Contents

To the Reader

Have you ever seen a factory? Perhaps you think that a silly question, like 'Have you ever seen a railway station?' because at the present day there is nearly always a factory of some sort in every town. You may pass a factory on your way home from school each day. Perhaps your father or an elder brother or sister works in one. It may be that you have been lucky enough to visit a biscuit factory or a chocolate factory as a member of a school party, and were allowed to sample the goods.

If you live in the Midlands or the North of England, I expect you will know that although a place where biscuits or shoes or jam or cameras are made is called a factory, a place where cloth or thread is manufactured is usually called a mill. At one time, in the early eighteenth century, about two hundred and fifty years ago, there were no factories as we know them today, but there were mills—windmills and water-mills for grinding corn. The very first factories were for making silk and cotton thread or yarn. The machinery in them was driven by a water-wheel, like the works of a flour-mill, so they were called mills also. We should call them textile mills because textiles means any kind of cloth or fabric or the thread from which it is made. The building of the mills and the invention of machines to work in them were the beginning of the change in industry which is known as the Industrial Revolution.

Words printed in *italics* are explained in the Glossary (pp. 107-108).

1. Making a Living the Old Way

One of the first places in the world to experience the changes brought about by the Industrial Revolution was Belper, in Derbyshire.

If you were to visit Belper today, you would probably come by road from Derby. Six miles from Derby, you would pass through Duffield village. Before the eighteenth century, Duffield was much more important than Belper. Duffield, however, had no part in the Industrial Revolution and, unlike Belper, it did not grow in the eighteenth and nineteenth centuries.

If you look at the map, you will see that the road next passes through Milford. Beside the road is the English Sewing Cotton Company's factory. The bridge which carries the road across the river Derwent was built about the same time as the cotton-mill.

About a mile further on we come to Belper, the road following the river valley, most of the houses and shops set on the hilly slope on the right hand side of the road. If we continue straight along Bridge Street we come to a fork in the road; one arm takes us to the bridge over the Derwent; the other leads out of Belper again and on to Cromford, Matlock and, if one goes far enough, to Manchester.

If you look at the map again you will see more cotton-mills near the bridge. Notice how the river is wider above the bridge. That is because the water is held back by a weir. This dam was created when the first cotton-mill was built, because it was worked by a water-wheel and a steady supply of water was necessary. Can you find, near the mills, a street called Long Row? The houses there were built for the people who worked in

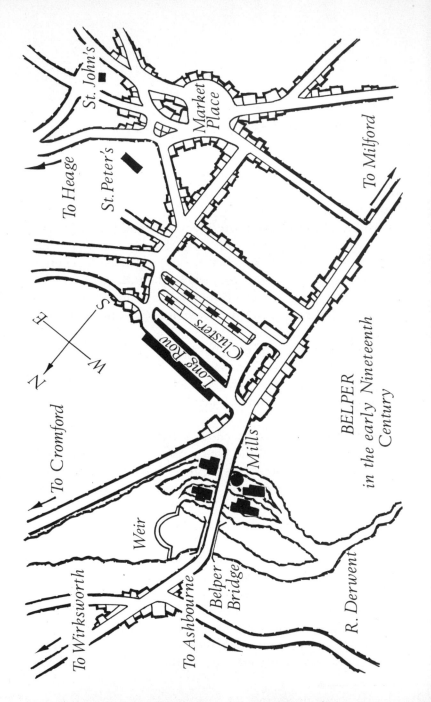

BELPER
in the early Nineteenth Century

St. John's

Market Place

St. Peter's

To Milford

To Heage

Long Row

Clusters

To Cromford

N E S W

Weir

Mills

To Wirksworth

To Ashbourne

Belper Bridge

R. Derwent

2

the mills. Look on the map for the present parish church of St Peter, which was not built until 1824, and the twelfth-century chapel of St John. From the twelfth to the eighteenth century this little church was the hub of the village, or rather villages, because up to the end of the eighteenth century there were three separate groups of houses with open land between.

The population of Belper in 1741 was 532; the number of houses 113. There was little or no growth until the last quarter of the eighteenth century when the cotton-mills were built. How did these hundred-odd families make a living before there were any factories for them to work in?

In spite of its smallness, Belper was already famous, or notorious, as the centre of a community of nailers, or nail-makers. The nailers of Belper and the neighbouring hamlets were a rough lot of people even by eighteenth-century standards. A history of Derbyshire, printed in Belper itself in 1811, described the town in the early eighteenth-century as having been 'as low in population as it was backward in *civility;* and considered as the *insignificant* residence of a few uncivilized nailers'.

Stealing was one sign of incivility. The Derbyshire Quarter Sessions Order Book mentions a case in 1733:
'Whereas Thos. Whitacre of Little Eaton in this County, Naylor, was *indicted* this Sessions for stealing hay, the Goods & Chattells of Wm. Stone and being found Guilty of the same, This Court doth order and it is hereby ordered That he be sent to the House of Correction at Derby . . . . and there whipt and kept to hard labour for the space of a Month next & that he find sufficient Surety for his good behaviour for seven years next ensuing.'

The nailers' womenfolk were just as likely to get on the wrong side of the law as the men. In 1743:
'Margaret Blood, Wife of Thomas Blood of Horsley in this County, Nailor, being Indicted at this Sessions for Stealing a parcell of wool . . . . was accordingly tryed and upon such tryal was found Guilty, whereupon this Court doth Order that the said Margaret Blood be sent to ye Goal for the County of Derby and whipt at Derby in the usual manner.'

Inside a nail shop

The value of the parcel of wool in this case was two shillings, so you might guess that it was not just greed but perhaps poverty which prompted this crime.

The nailers, like most working people in the eighteenth century, lived from week to week and from day to day, always on the edge of poverty. Long hours of hard work alternated with periods of idleness.

The making of the nails was done in a nailshop, a small shed built on to the end of the cottage or standing by itself in the cottage garden. The nailshop contained a hearth and bellows and an anvil. Each nailer was given a quantity of iron in the form of rods by the nail-master for whom he worked. These rods were weighed carefully before being handed over on a Saturday for the nailer to trundle home in his barrow. The rods were made into nails during the week by cutting, heating and hammering, and the nails were taken back to the nail-master's warehouse on the following Saturday, when the nail-maker was paid for the work he had done. The nails he handed over were

Old nail shop, Joseph Street, Belper

weighed, and the weight checked against the recorded weight
of the original iron rods. For every 56 lbs of rods 45 lb of nails
had to be returned. If the nails were short weight, some of the
man's wage was deducted; and if there was a serious difference
in weight, the nailer might find himself in trouble with the law.

On Thursday, 22 October 1778, the Derby Mercury
reported:

'Tuesday was committed to the County Goal, by Brabazon
Hallows, Esq., one of his Majesty's Justices of the Peace,
Richard Milward and John Watson of Belpar, Nail-makers,
charged with *purloining* and *embezzling* a Quantity of Iron, the
Property of Mr. John Wilkinson, of Belpar aforesaid.'

This was a very serious charge, and if they had been proved
guilty, they would probably have been transported to a convict
settlement. You may be relieved to know that they were
discharged a week later by the Justice of the Peace who had put
them in prison.

A nailer prided himself on his independence and, in some

ways, he was his own boss. He worked at home in his own nail-shop. As they generally worked in pairs or threes, he might take and change partners or hire his own assistant. He used his own equipment and tools, and he chose his own hours of work. He did not have to begin and end work at a set time.

Almost all nailers had the habit of keeping St Monday. This meant spending the day as a holiday, usually in the ale-house, drinking and gambling or just gossiping with his mates. This was sometimes prolonged for a second day or more, especially if trade was good, the demand for nails high and the nailmasters anxious not to lose any of their men. Farey, the surveyor, describes how when trade was brisk the nailmasters would be persuaded to give their men an advance of wages, in effect a loan, part of which would have to be carried on to the next week, when again a further advance would be expected:

'Frequently Saint Monday, Saint Tuesday, and, perhaps Saint Wednesday also had been religiously worshipped in the Ale-house, and few, if any, Nails had then been made; and when Saturday night came, a part only of the Wednesday advance could be set off, without instantly losing the Man; and the same again next week, and so on, until many of the best Nailers were 20 pounds in debt to their Masters.'

Nailers and others on 'St Monday'

When trade was slack, however, the nailmasters might be unable to supply any iron, much less offer an advance of wages and the debt was a burden which could not easily be got rid of.

Another industry which was carried on in and around Belper was stocking-making or framework-knitting. This industry was much more widespread than nail-making. It was carried on in the three Midland counties of Leicester, Nottingham and Derby. The hand-worked machine, the stocking-frame, was about the same size as a small loom—as big as a writing bureau. It was used not only for knitting stockings but also for caps, gloves, mufflers and for shaped pieces which could be sewn together or seamed to make other garments. Wool, silk or cotton-yarn could be used. Wool was usually used in Leicestershire, silk in Derbyshire and cotton in Nottinghamshire. As Belper was almost the same distance from both Derby and Nottingham, the framework-knitters of Belper and the neighbouring hamlets used either silk or cotton.

A framework knitter

The framework-knitters, like the nailers, and like most industrial workers in the eighteenth century, worked at home. Houses or cottages were sometimes built with an extra-wide window in the top floor room so that the knitter, or stockinger, would have plenty of light on his work. A stockinger was supplied with yarn by the hosier who employed him. Like the nailers' iron rods, this was weighed. The knitted garments were also weighed when the stockinger returned them to the hosier, and any difference in weight had to be accounted for. Only one quarter of an ounce wastage was allowed on every pound of yarn. The hosier then paid the stockinger's wages and gave out more yarn.

As for the tools of the trade, we have seen that the nailers owned their own anvil, hammers, etc. But these were fairly cheap and would last many years. A stocking-frame was expensive. Between 1780 and 1810 a new frame cost from £25 to £50 depending on its size and quality. A second-hand frame could be bought for about £10, but this was still more money than a stockinger was likely to have. Wages in the same period amounted to about 15s a week, out of which only a few pence could be saved. Most of the stockingers hired or rented the frames from their employer, the hosier. Frame rent varied from 9d to 2s per week and sometimes this had to be paid even if trade was slack and the hosier was not supplying any yarn to be knitted.

Another industry which gave employment to a few men in Belper and its neighbourhood in the eighteenth century was coal-mining. Belper is on the extreme Western edge of the Midland coalfield and the seams of coal, though near the surface, were very thin and poor. Mostly they were worked by single families who dug a hundredweight or two at a time for their own use or for sale locally.

An incident reported to the Court of Quarter Sessions at Chesterfield in 1748 illustrates both the fact that coal was being obtained in Belper, and the rather alarming disregard for ordinary 'law and order' in a very backward part of Derbyshire in the mid-eighteenth century:

'The Jurors for our Sovereign Lord the King upon their Oath

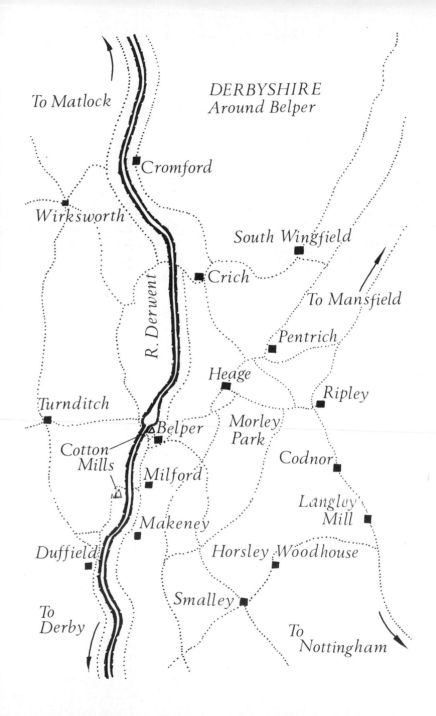

present that William Blount, late of Heage in the County of Derby, Labourer, on the first day of September . . . . upon a certain part of the King's Highway there called Belper Ward, lying between the Town of Belper and the Town of Heage, used for all the Kings Subjects with their Horses, Coaches, Carts and Carriages to go upon ride pass and labour at their will and pleasure, unlawfully and injuriously did dig and cause to be digged several pits or Shafts for getting and drawing up Coals, each containing in circumference eight foot . . .'

In other words, the enterprising William Blount was digging great holes in the road to get at the coal beneath. In spite of the wording of the complaint we may guess that in fact very few people used the road with coaches, carts and carriages, or the accused would not have been able to do so much apparently uninterrupted digging.

Pits in less unusual places, of course, continued to be worked, and helped a few people to make a living.

There was also a small local pottery industry but this supported only the members of one family and a few workmen.

These were the industries of Belper in the early eighteenth century. Most people worked long hours, twelve or more a day but in good times they could earn enough to live on by working five days a week or even less. Even working six days a week, they usually had strength enough to amuse themselves energetically.

A writer in 1660 noted that: 'The common people will endure long and hard labour insomuch that after twelve hours work they will go in the evening to football, stockball, prison base, wrestling, cricket, cudgel-playing or some such like *vehement* exercise for their recreation.'

James Harrison, one of the family of Belper nailmasters, mentions in his diary in 1735: 'Had my ankle sprained with wrestling with Obadiah Flint.' He was then thirty-three years of age. Four years later he records taking part in foot races: 'Run on Belper Ward the famous Merry-Tow and won a guinea; five guineas; a saddle above forty pound; and more prizes.'

10   An entry in his diary tells us something of what football

Playing leap-frog

could be like. Notice that the players each contributed towards the prize fund:

'Three hateful football matches betwixt Duffield and Belper. First about Christmas for 5s per man; six players; won by Belper on Wednesday, February 2, 1732, won by Duffield. Belper 'twas thought play'd Butty (that is, had been bribed to play badly on purpose and lose the game. This annoyed the spectators who had placed bets on Belper to win):
A *prodigious* fight followed, the like never seen in this or perhaps in ye last; abundance of broken heads.'

Around Christmas and the New Year, the boys and young men of the town would go round *guising* or *mumming*. The central character in the mime was dressed in a sheepskin as 'the Derby Ram', accompanied by 'the butcher' with a huge wooden knife. At each house, the ram was killed and miraculously revived while the group sang some of the song of the Derby Ram:

As I was going to Derby, Sir,
All on a market day
I met the finest Ram, Sir,
That ever was fed on hay.

This Ram was fat behind, Sir,
This Ram was fat before,
This Ram was ten yards high, Sir,
Indeed he was no more.

The Wool upon his back, Sir,
Reached up into the sky,
The Eagles made their nests there,
For I heard their young ones cry.

Daddle-i-day, daddle-i-day,
Fal-de-ral, fal-de-ral, daddle-i-day.

The people of the house were then expected to hand around fruit, nuts, or coppers.

For less energetic entertainment, the nailers and their fellow villagers would have to go to Derby, in a waggon, on a hired horse perhaps, or tramping the eight miles on foot.

There they might see a play performed by a travelling company of actors.

The whipping of convicted men and women in Derby market-place provided free 'entertainment', but was too commonplace to be worth while travelling eight muddy miles to see.

Less expensive than stage plays but more unusual than public punishments were the 'peepshows' often given at an inn.

At the Red Lion Inn could be seen an American Elk. He was to be on show for two days only 'because his horns grow so fast'. The charges for admission in this case were 'Ladies and Gentlemen 6d. Children and Servants 3d'.

James Harrison wrote in his diary in 1743:
'An Easter Fair at the Vergin's Inn in Derby. For 6d I saw the following show; (viz.)—A large old Lyon into whose mouth the Keeper put his head and shouted down his throat. 2. A fine young Lyon. 3. A large old Leopard whose tail I took hold of. 4. A beautiful young Leopard; A Mountain Catt from Jamaica as

bigg as a Bull Dogg. A Onuss or Civet Catt very sleepy and sweet; a very fine Tyger, an exceeding fierce beast called ye Hyena or Jena—ye Man Eater. 9. A Wolfe. 10. A Jacall, very fierce and several monkeys, apes, etc. the finest show ever seen.'

Fun on the ice

Certainly we should agree, a show worth the journey from Belper and worth a hard-earned sixpence to see it. The problem might, of course, be to get the sixpence.

Often there were no nails to be made because trade was slack. The hosiers might not be putting out work for several weeks at a time. Then the people must turn their hands to some other work if they could find it. If their employer felt a sense of responsibility himself, he might try to help them.

13

B

In most cases, however, when an employer stopped giving out work for any reason, he made no attempt to help the men or women who were turned off.

Luckily, most families in the eighteenth century did not depend entirely on the father's weekly wage of a single job.

A 'For Sale' notice in the 'Derby Mercury' of 29 December 1776, illustrates the various ways of making a living. Horsley Woodhouse is about three miles from Belper:

'To BE SOLD

'Three Cottages or Dwelling-Houses situate at Hill-Top near Horsley-Woodhouse, Derbyshire, one of which is a Public House, with an Orchard and Gardens to the same, and other convenient Buildings adjoining; consisting of a Stocking-Weaver's, Blacksmith's and Nailor's Shops, with a Cowhouse and Pigsties, all Freehold.'

We can picture a family occupying a cottage such as these. Sam Ward, the father, is a nailer, that is, he spends most of his time in the nail shop, but he also gives several hours a week to the garden, where he has a couple of apple trees and a large potato patch as well as peas, beans and other crops. Jacob, the eldest son, is in his twenties, and works with his father in his nailshop. He helps in the garden also, but his main job is looking after the pigs. These are bought as piglets each year, fattened, and sold to a butcher. One or two are slaughtered and the meat salted and kept.

Sam's wife, Martha, was apprenticed as a framework-knitter when young and owns her own frame. She is sometimes given a few days' work by a Nottingham hosier. Now and then she buys some yarn from a travelling 'bag hosier' and sells any stockings that she knits over and above her family's needs. She has taught her fifteen year old daughter, Margaret, to use the frame so that she divides her time, like her mother, between housework and knitting.

The younger children cannot yet do much to add to the family's income. Isaac, aged ten, is often in the nailshop with his father and elder brother, but is still too young to be much real help. He and Dick, his eight year old brother, go round the hedges and corners of the sheds and garden twice a day to collect any eggs laid by the half-dozen hens which scratch and cluck half-wild around the place. From the open land around, they bring back sticks for the fire, which helps to save a few pence. Five year old Mary, the baby of the family, is no help at all, but looks forward to the time when she will be old enough to start learning to use her mother's stocking-frame.

All these activities were necessary if the family was to live fairly comfortably. Cultivating a garden, and keeping pigs or poultry were not merely hobbies for pleasure or to earn extra money to buy luxuries. Everything and everybody had to help just to provide the rent and the necessary food and clothing. If any of the main sources of income stopped, if working members of the family fell ill, then there would be real hardship. Threadbare clothes would have to be made to last longer; fires would have to be smaller or gone without, and there would be less food.

What poor people ate has been described by Sir Frederick Eden, who conducted a survey in 1797. One of the commonest dishes for the poorest was 'hasty pudding, which is made of oatmeal, water and salt, about 13 oz of meal to a quart of water, which is sufficient for a meal for two labourers. It is eaten with a little milk or beer poured upon it, or with a little cold butter put into the middle, or with a little treacle.'

This was something like porridge, flavoured according to one's taste. Potatoes were also very popular: 'Potatoes are not only particularly good in the North of England but used in various ways.' Apart from being roasted or boiled, and eaten with butter, they were often

'. . . boiled, chopped into small pieces and eaten with butter (either cold or melted) or bacon fried; but the principal way in which they are used by labourers' families in the North is by being peeled, or rather scraped raw, chopped, and boiled together with a small quantity of meat cut into very small pieces. The whole of this mixture is then formed into a hash, with pepper, salt, onions, etc.'

Perhaps you think this sounds more appetizing than hasty pudding, especially if the quantity of meat was not so very small.

Food prices locally were as follows:

flour   2s 2d to 2s 9d   the stone

oatmeal	2s 4d	the stone
potatoes	10d	the peck
butter	9d	the lb
milk	1½d to 2d	the quart
beef	4d to 5d	the lb
mutton	5d	the lb
veal	4d	the lb
bacon	7d to 8d	the lb
eggs	3 for 2d	

A workman might earn anything from 5s to 15s or, in some cases, up to 20s a week, depending on the kind of work he did, his skill and how long he was able or willing to work. Take a family like the one we have described and see how you would do the housekeeping for a week. You will see what a difference it could make if the family grew their own potatoes, and produced bacon and eggs at home, instead of having to buy them.

A family like Sam Ward's could weather a bad patch for a week or two, but many families were less well-off and had fewer

A poor woman

working members and more small children. What could they do when there was no work and starvation faced them? The only thing for it was to go to the overseer of the poor and ask for money to help them out for a week, a month, or more, until the nail trade or the stocking industry took a turn for the better.

In the eighteenth century, each parish had an Overseer of the Poor, whose job it was to distribute the money—the Poor Rate—which the wealthier citizens had to pay. The overseers were supervised by the county authorities, the Justices of the Peace, who sometimes ordered money to be paid to a certain person. The J.P.s meeting in the Court of Quarter Sessions at Easter in 1712 ordered: 'that the overseer of the poor of Belper in this County do pay unto Mary Porter of Belper aforesaid two shillings and sixpence weekly out of the money raised, or to be raised, for the necessary relief of the poor there, for the maintenance of herself and four children.'

While the overseers for each parish normally paid out as they thought fit to their own poor, they were anxious not to have to support the poor of a neighbouring parish. Often a legal tussle took place between the overseers of neighbouring parishes over which parish a person or a poor family had the right to claim relief from.

Orphans who had to be looked after by the parish were apprenticed if it were at all possible. Although there were no gilds as in the Middle Ages, apprenticeship as a way of learning a trade was still the usual practice in the eighteenth century.

Generally, apprentices were children or young people who were 'put apprentice' by their parents. The craftsman who took them had to be paid a fee, which varied according to his trade and his importance. The usual term of apprenticeship was seven years. On the one side, the master got his fee, plus unpaid assistance in his trade; on the other, the apprentice got his food and lodging and clothing for seven years plus training in a job at which he could later earn a living.

There was a written agreement, called an *indenture*, which stated exactly what the master and the apprentice had to do. On 17 October 1720, Samuel Tarrat, a labourer's son, was apprenticed to a tailor, Joseph Barker, of Kirk Ireton, near

Rich and poor children

Belper. The apprenticeship was to last for seven years:

'During which said Terme ye said apprentice his said master faithfully shall serve, his secrets keepe, his Commandments Lawful and Honest everywhere doo. Hee shall not damidge, nor see itt to be done of others, but the same to his power shall hinder, or shall forthwith warn his said master thereof.'

The apprentice was to avoid damaging his master's good name by mixing in low company.

'Taverns or Ale Houses he shall not haunt or frequent: at Cards, Dice or other unlawful games he shall not play: from his serviss aforesaid he shall not depart nor absent himself by day or night without ye Lycence of said master: but in all things as a good and Lawful Apprentice he shall justly and truely demean and behave himself unto his said Master. . . .'

Joseph Barker undertook to:

'Teach Instruct and Inform . . . . after the best manner that he can, with a due manner of *Chastisement*: And shall give and Provide to and for his said Apprentice, good and sufficient Meat and Drinck and Lodging, fit for such an apprentice during all ye said Terme.'

Samuel's father, however, agreed that he would: 'find and provide for his son all his wearing Apparell, Both Woollen and Linnen.' The indenture specified that the fee was to be paid in four annual instalments of seven shillings and sixpence each. Notice, by the way, that Samuel's clothes are woollen and linen. This was 1720 and cotton was not commonly worn at that time. What do you think would be considered 'a due manner of chastisement' in the early eighteenth century?

Parish authorities apprenticed poor orphans, or children whose parents depended on poor relief, whenever they could. They were required by law to see that such children learnt a trade, but they were often more concerned with getting the children off the list of those who had to be maintained. Boys were often apprenticed for a small fee to farmers as labourers, and girls as domestic servants. In both cases, they were often merely treated as cheap labour and learnt very little that was of any use to them.

This, then, was Belper in the mid-eighteenth century. About 500 people, most of them quite poor, having enough to live on, but no more. Their work was not regular, their wages were not certain. At any time, a loss of orders for nails, a change of fashion in stockings, might mean a flock of people with large families going to the parish overseer to ask for money.

Although it was poor and isolated, Belper did have certain things which could be valuable if anyone could put them to good use. There was the river Derwent flowing briskly past the town; there was plenty of wood and building stone. There was also the skill of the people—of the nailers in working with iron, of the stockingers in handling silk and cotton yarn and using the quite complicated stocking frames. There were also the children of the town who, because of the character of the trades, were unable to do much towards earning their keep. They would be willing to work at any job which would bring in a little money to help the family income. But up to 1776 there were no jobs to be had.   19

2 Building the Mills

On Friday, 13 December 1771, the following advertisement appeared in the 'Derby Mercury', the county paper:

'COTTON MILL, CROMFORD. 10th December 1771.

'WANTED Immediately, two Journeymen Clock-Makers, or others that understands Tooth and Pinion well: Also a Smith that can forge and file.—Likewise two Wood Turners that have been accustomed to Wheel-making, *Spole*-turning, &c. Weavers residing in this Neighbourhood, by applying at the Mill, may have good Work. There is Employment at the above Place, for Women, Children, &c, and good Wages.

'N.B. A Quantity of Box Wood is wanted:

'Any Persons whom the above may suit, will be treated with by Messrs. Arkwright and Co. at the Mill, or Mr Strutt, in Derby.'

Jedediah Strutt

This mill, advertising for workers, was the first water-powered cotton-mill in England. Cromford is about eight miles farther up the Derwent valley from Belper. You will notice that the owners of the mill were the business partners, Richard Arkwright and Jedediah Strutt.

Arkwright, whom you can find out more about in a later chapter, was a Lancashire man, who had come to Nottingham in 1768, bringing with him the idea of a new machine for spinning cotton. Jedediah Strutt was a hosier from Derby. He had invented a gadget to fit on an ordinary stocking-frame for doing ribbed knitting, and he had a prosperous business in Derby.

When they met, Arkwright had the idea of having his machines driven by water-power and he and Strutt decided to build the mill at Cromford.

You can easily guess why they needed men who understood how to make gears, smiths and wood-turners. Weavers were needed, as they understood about yarn. Notice also the offer of employment for women and children.

This mill was such a success that in 1776 Arkwright and Strutt began to build, not one other mill, but two. One of these was again at Cromford, but Belper was chosen as the site for the other. What was this mill like and how was it built? We had better say first that within a fairly short time, Jedediah Strutt and his sons had not one mill but several. (The partnership with Arkwright was dissolved in 1781.)

The building of the first mill in Belper, the South Mill, was started, as we have seen, in 1776 and it was working by 1778. Already before its completion, Jedediah had bought some existing industrial buildings at Milford, about a mile and a half downstream from Belper. These had been advertised for sale in the 'Birmingham Gazette' in April, 1777:

'IRONWORKS

'To be sold, New Mills and Mackenay Forges (Milford and Makeney) in the Parish of Duffield and County of Derby, most beautifully and conveniently situated upon each side of the River Derwent; consisting of two Iron Forges; Hammersman's Forge with a Scrap Furnace, and *divers* Workmen's Houses, Gardens, and a spacious Yard . . . The Situation of these Works, with the constant Power of the Water, and all their Conveniences renders them capable of being vastly improved, and altered or changed to any other Purpose or Business whatever, where a continual Supply of Water is necessary . . .'

Strutt would have heard locally that these works were for sale, and he bought them. Why do you think he was interested in buying iron forges when his business was hosiery and cotton-spinning? He could, of course, as the advertisement suggested, alter them to suit his purpose. In cotton-spinning by machine, a continual supply of water was certainly necessary. You might not guess, however, that he could use iron forges for making the rods, bolts, screws, plates, brackets, etc., which were needed in building his mill and in building the machines to put in it. Nowadays, a company starting a factory pays a building firm to put up the premises and buys the machines from an engineering firm. In 1776, Strutt had to design his own mill, hire workmen himself to build it, and other craftsmen to build the machines.

Jedediah began building a cotton-mill at Milford about 1780,

Milford Mills

and a second mill in Belper in 1784 which was working by 1786. Skilled workers were hard to get and he was advertising in the 'Derby Mercury' on 3 October 1781:

'WANTED

'Two or Three JOINERS and One or Two SMITHS, of good Character and good Workmen.—Apply to the Cotton-Mills at Belper, or to Mr STRUTT, Derby.'

Again on 29 May 1783, he advertised vacancies for 'several STONE-MASONS and BRICKLAYERS, that are good Workmen' at New Mills (Milford).

The masons and bricklayers were needed for building or alterations to existing buildings. The joiners and smiths were necessary for constructing and maintaining the machines which were at this time largely made of wood.

Only six years after the completion of the North Mill in Belper in 1786, Strutt was putting up a new warehouse in Milford and yet another mill in Belper, the West Mill, which was working in 1796. Jedediah himself died in 1797, but his sons continued to run the mills as a family business.

It was obviously prospering. A schoolmaster in the town wrote to a former pupil who had emigrated to America: 'Messrs Strutts go on swimmingly—they are erecting a very large mill at Belper; and Mr George is beginning to build himself a noble house on the bridge hill.' (George Strutt was one of Jedediah's Sons.)

This was not the end of the mill-building, however. In 1803 the North Mill was burnt down—a fairly common happening in the early days of cotton-mills. The 'Derby Mercury' printed an account of the fire on Wednesday, 12 January 1803:

'About three o'clock this morning a most tremendous fire broke out in one of the large Cotton-Mills belonging to Messrs. Strutt, at Belper, in this county, which raged with incredible fury, and in a few hours destroyed it, with all the valuable machinery, waterwheel, &c. The cause of this dreadful accident is not yet known. The loss will be immense, as no part of the property is insured.'

Rebuilding began almost immediately and the new North Mill was in production in the following year, 1804. Between then and 1810 work was begun on three more buildings at Milford and Belper. In 1810 the original Mill built by Jedediah in 1776 was pulled down and a larger and more modern South Mill was built on the same site and was working in 1812.

The second North Mill

So within about thirty-five years, no less than eleven separate buildings had been put up at Belper and Milford. A boy or girl of ten in 1776, old enough to take an interest in the building of the first mill (and old enough to work in it) would still be living and working when the last one was completed.

What sort of buildings then were these first cotton-mills? One of them, the North Mill, is still standing, so that any visitor to Belper can see for himself. It still houses machinery and is used by the present firm, the English Sewing Cotton Company, the successors to the Strutt's family business. Other much later buildings stand beside it; one very large block opened in 1912 overshadows it and across the road there is an even more recent section of the Company's works built in 1960. The early buildings at Milford were still standing until a few years ago also, when they were pulled down. Some of the floors were unsafe but the walls needed a heavy battering from the iron ball of the demolition crane before they came crashing down.

There are some late eighteenth-century and early nineteenth-century mills still standing in other parts of England, sometimes in quite unexpected places, but most of our knowledge of what the early mills were like comes from contemporary descriptions and plans, building account books, and pictures.

They were not very large places, to our way of thinking, but to people at the time they were larger than any building they had ever seen, except perhaps a cathedral or the stately home of some rich gentleman. The Strutt's West Mill in Belper was 200 feet long, 30 feet wide and six storeys high. The second South Mill of 1811-12 was 118 feet long, 40 feet wide and had five storeys and an attic under the roof. For comparison, St Paul's Cathedral, London, is 515 feet long and the nave is 40 feet wide. The frontage of Kedleston Hall, one of the great houses of Derbyshire, is 360 feet. The little church of St John in Belper is only 72 feet long and 24 feet wide.

Belper and Milford Mills

A cotton-mill of the eighteenth or early nineteenth century was solidly built of brick or stone, or both. Sometimes stone was used for the foundations and lower courses, especially if in contact with the water, and brick used for the rest of the walls. Besides this, large amounts of timber, iron, lead and glass were required. Most of the building materials were bought and brought to the site in an unprepared state and were cut and shaped on the spot. Strutt's accounts for the building of the West Mill in 1792-95 contain the following entries:

	£	s	d
3 Labourers altering scaffold poles	2	8	0
Brags & nails used for braces & scaffolding..		5	10
1822 feet inch deal boards for gutters, and lineing about trap doors and sky lights @ 1½d	11	7	9
52 sheets of Lead for gutters			
138 c 3 qr 0 lb @ 19s	131	16	3
345200 bricks @ 21s per thousand	362	9	2½
4 Cast pillars 14 c 3 qr 8 lb @ 12s 3d ..	9	1	6¾
Digging 3 holes for foundations of Pillars in Counting House		7	6
Pots for the Top Storey			
35609 @ 52s 6d	93	9	5½
Carriage of Pots from the Pot House ..		6	0
Pots for arching 3900	10	4	9

The '4 Cast pillars' were cast-iron pillars, of course, but what do you make of 'Pots for the Top Storey'? Not chimney pots, because the number given is over thirty-five thousand! The last entry quoted might give you a clue. The pots were used for making the floor.

A great danger in early cotton-mills was fire. Belper North Mill, you will remember, was burnt down in 1803. There was usually a good deal of fluff and dust in the air, settling on everything. There was oil from the machines, and oil-rags. There was cotton waste, odds and ends of raw cotton and cotton yarn. All these caught fire very easily, and if a fire accidentally started, a timber-floored building would burn quickly and fiercely.

The Strutts were anxious to lessen the danger by reducing the amount of timber used in the building. This was done from 1792

A floor pot

onwards by having brick vaults or arches for the floor between each storey, and pots for the floor of the top storey. These pots were rather like squat flower-pots four inches in diameter and five inches high. They were set in plaster with the narrow end down to give the correct amount of curve to the vault. The tops were closed with an earthenware lid and the floor above built up level with mortar. This gave a light top floor, not strong enough to bear the weight of machines, but enough for the top storey to be used for storage, or, as in the case of the North Mill, as a schoolroom for the child workers.

Pots like these had been used in the Palais Royal theatre in Paris in 1790, and William Strutt had asked for some to be sent to him from France, but whether the samples ever arrived in England we do not know.

Cast-iron pillars or columns gave support down the middle of the mill through each storey, and at first, in the 1792 buildings, the timber beams between these columns were covered with thin sheets of iron. When the North Mill was rebuilt after the fire, William Strutt used iron beams instead of timber. At this time, he was exchanging ideas about iron-framed buildings with Charles Bage, an engineer who had built an iron-framed flax-mill in Shrewsbury in 1797, and with the well-known firm of Boulton and Watt. Good quality iron was essential for the columns and beams, but with brick or pot floors such buildings were practically fireproof. These mills were the forerunners of the modern steel-framed skyscraper blocks of offices or flats.

27

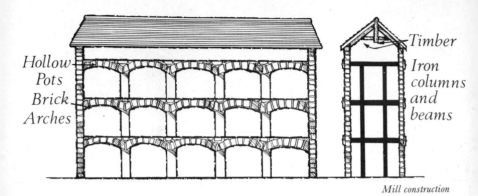

Hollow Pots Brick Arches

Timber

Iron columns and beams

Mill construction

The roads around Belper were busy in 1792, with a never-ending stream of carts and waggons bringing materials to the mill site. Much of the stone and timber was obtained from land which the Strutt family had bought in the neighbourhood. The only timbers used in the main construction were those supporting the roof. The iron beams and columns were brought from Chesterfield but there were brickyards only a mile or two from the site. The pots were also made locally. John Farey, an engineer and surveyor, listing pottery works in Derbyshire in 1811 makes a special mention of: 'Smalley Common, Water-pipes and Cylinders for arched, fire-proof Ceilings.'

The building of the mill itself was only part, if the main part, of the work to be done. The machines had to be constructed and installed, each connected by a belt and pulley to a drive-shaft. These ran overhead the length of each storey and all worked off a vertical drive-shaft which was geared to the water-wheel.

If you have seen a corn-mill, you will know how a water-wheel works. The wheels which drove spinning machinery had to be much larger, however. The two wheels of the West Mill were described by a visitor in 1802 as being forty and forty-eight feet long and eighteen feet and twelve feet in diameter. The shafts, or axles, of these wheels were made of separate timbers and were hollow and hooped with iron like a barrel. One axle was five to six feet and the other eight to nine feet in diameter. An entry in the accounts reads: 'Iron for hooping the Shaft 44 c 0 qr 21 lb

@ 22s £48 12s 1½d and £1 3s 4d was spent on tar to paint the wheel.

This was in 1795. Later, the original timber wheels were replaced by iron ones. Stephen Glover writing about the mills (as all visitors to Belper did) about 1830 reports that the mills were worked by eleven water-wheels 'principally composed of iron. Two of these were built by Mr T. C. Hewes of Manchester and the other nine by Messrs Strutt.'

These lighter and more durable iron wheels, like the iron beams used in the building, were made possible only by improvements in iron manufacture and iron working during the eighteenth century.

Excavations for the channel or 'cut' to lead water from the river Derwent to the West Mill continued from May 1794 to January 1795. The walling of this and the tunnel under the road with masonry continued into 1796. You will see from the map that the highway ran between the West Mill and the earlier buildings, and that the road crosses the river very near to the mills, by Belper Bridge. Workmen working at this difficult job, often having to stand up to their knees or deeper in water, were paid extra, as danger money, and were sometimes provided with free ale to encourage them. Their wages ranged from about 1s to 2s 6d per day according to their skill and experience.

To add to the difficulties, a flood damaged the old Belper Bridge so badly in 1795 that the County authorities decided to have a new one. Thomas Sykes, the County Surveyor, was able to record in his notebook: 'May 25th, 1796, the first stoone of Belper Bridge whas laid in South bank pear.'

You can imagine a great deal of confusion and bustle of stonemasons and waggoners, horses, carts, piles of stone and timber cluttering up the road and the river banks. The Surveyor was careful to note that Isaac and Benjamin Marshall, the contractors, agree 'to be at the expense of providing and paying damage to the owners of grounds adjoining, for laying down materials'.

For all kinds of water-mills, a weir—in effect a low dam—is necessary to hold back the water of the river and create a reservoir. Water from this is drawn off to the cuts leading to

C

A road waggon

the wheels through sluice-gates. By opening the sluice-gates little or much the flow of water to the wheel is regulated, and the wheel revolves at a constant speed.

The Strutt's weir was, and still is, quite an impressive sight. By 1820, the river above the weir had been spread out beyond its original banks to cover an extra fourteen acres. Look at the map and see how much wider it is upstream from the mills. John Farey, writing in 1817, was full of admiration for the work which had been done:

'From the Bridge upwards, the Derwent has been widened; projecting angles, Trees, Alder-stems, and all other impediments to the free course of the floods have been removed by those most spirited and judicious improvers, Messrs. Strutts, whose Weirs, Flood-gates, etc. give a more perfect command of this large and very variable River, for the use of their Cotton-Mills, than can perhaps anywhere else be witnessed. The sides of the River, as far as it acts as a Dam, have been walled in great part, and in order to

30

prevent any ill effects from the penning of the River by their Weir (on pretence of which, several most vexatious actions were a few years ago maintained against them) a capacious brick barrel arch has been carried from below the Bridge, on the West side of the River, for a quarter of a mile or more, to receive the land and soakage waters.'

These were some of the first problems; designing the building, getting the workmen to build it, obtaining the right materials and providing for the water supply to drive the machines.

From 1771 onwards, cotton-mills were going up all over Derbyshire as other men followed the example of Arkwright and Strutt. In 1817, John Farey counted 115 spinning-mills in Derbyshire alone, and there were many more in Lancashire and Cheshire. There were also mills for weaving cotton-cloth by that time, and mills for spinning and weaving wool, mainly in the West Riding of Yorkshire.

Of course, as soon as a mill was built and the machines were installed, people were needed to work at the cotton-spinning. The Strutts had about six hundred workers in their two Belper mills in 1789. By 1833, they were employing about two thousand people in Belper and a further seven hundred to eight hundred in Milford. You will read in the next chapter how so many workers were obtained and what it was like to work in an early cotton-mill.

3 Working in the Mills

Most of the workers in an early cotton-mill were children, because children's fingers were nimble, to tie or 'piece' together
threads which broke on the machines; and children were small
enough to crawl behind and under the machines to clean them.
It was also easier to make children rather than adult workers
keep hard at work and obey the factory rules.

How could a cotton manufacturer who had just built a new mill
obtain perhaps one hundred or more children to work for him?

Can you remember, from the first chapter, the poor children who were looked after by the parish overseers, and were, if possible, apprenticed to some master? The parish authorities had always found it difficult to get all of them off their hands (and off the parish rates). Here was one answer to the difficulty of both the overseers who had too many children and the factory owner who needed child-workers. Since large numbers of children were needed, they were obtained from parishes in large towns, from which batches of twenty or more could be got at one time. Some Derbyshire mills had parish apprentices from Hull, from Edinburgh, and from London.

Parish apprentices

One apprentice from the parish of St Pancras in London told his story to John Brown of Manchester, who wrote it down in 1828.

His name was Robert Blincoe. He was born about the year 1792, and was put in St Pancras parish workhouse in 1796 as an orphan. In 1799, when Robert was about seven years old, the parish authorities arranged with the Lambert brothers, who owned a mill at Lowdham in Nottinghamshire, to transfer eighty children. The children had an uncomfortable four-day journey

33

to Nottingham in covered waggons, and were then taken on to the mill in carts. When the first cart, in which was young Blincoe, drove up to the door, a number of villagers flocked around. Blincoe heard them talking like this:

'God help the poor wretches.'

'Eh,' said another, 'what a fine collection of children, little do they know to what a life of slavery they are doomed.'

'The Lord have mercy upon them,' said a third.

'They'll find little mercy here,' said a fourth.

The eighty new arrivals were taken into a room with 'long narrow deal tables and wooden benches'. Here they were given supper of thin milk porridge 'of a very blue complexion' and black bread. While Blincoe and the others were half-heartedly eating, the parish children who were already apprenticed there came in. Blincoe noticed their dirty unkempt appearance, and their bare feet, and wondered why they were all staring intently at a hatch door in one wall:

'At a signal given the apprentices rushed to this door, and each, as he made his way, received his portion and withdrew to his place at the table. Blincoe was startled, seeing the boys pull out the fore-part of their shirts, and holding it up with both hands, received the hot boiled potatoes allotted for their supper. The girls held up their dirty greasy aprons that were saturated with grease and dirt . . . . Next the hungry crew ran to the tables of the newcomers, and voraciously devoured every crust of bread and every drop of porridge they had left . . . '

The newcomers were then herded off to the bedrooms, where they slept as best they could in double bunk-beds. The clanging of the factory bell woke them up at five o'clock the next morning, and they were turned out of their beds by the apprentice-master, or governor: 'The iron door of the chamber, creaking upon its hinges was opened, and in came the terrific governor, with the horse whip in his hand, and every boy hastily tumbled out of his crib, and huddled on his clothes with all possible haste.'

After porridge and black bread for breakfast, they began work in the mill at 5.30. They worked on without a break until mid-day, and after dinner had another seven or eight hours' work to do.

Once Blincoe got a hand caught in a machine, and lost the top joint of the forefinger on his left hand. When it had been bandaged, he had to go back and continue his work. The children were often punched or kicked or beaten by the overseers, and Robert realised why:

'The overlooker, who had charge of him, had a certain quantity of work to perform in a given time. If every child did not perform his allotted task, the fault was imputed to his overlooker, and he was discharged,—on the other hand, a *premium* was given if the full quantity of work was done, and not otherwise.'

Not surprisingly, Robert ran away but was caught and brought back, and soundly beaten. After he had been there three years, the mill closed down and the apprentices were transferred to another mill.

Looking back in 1828 the grown-up Robert Blincoe considered that he and his companions could have been worse off:

'They were kept decently clad, had a bettermost suit reserved for Sundays and holidays—were occasionally allowed a little time for play in the open air, and upon Goose Fair day the whole of them were conveyed in carts to Nottingham, and regaled with *furmenty;* and sixpence in money was allowed to the very youngest! They went pretty regularly to Lowdham Church on Sundays.'

There was nothing unusual in Robert and his fellow apprentices being transferred from one mill to another. Notices like the following frequently appeared in newspapers of the time:

'TO COTTON SPINNERS

'To be disposed of by Assignment, about twenty Girls (Apprentices) from 16 to 19 years of age.

'Apply personally or if by Letter, post paid, to B. Smart, in nr Warwick.'

Robert was disposed of by the Lamberts to the mill belonging to Ellis Needham, at Litton, in Derbyshire. The author of Blincoe's story had this to say about it: 'In the mill, where Blinco was next consigned, the parish children were considered, treated and consumed as a part of the raw materials; their strength, their marrow, their lives were consumed and converted into money, and as their live stock consisting of parish apprentices, diminished, new flocks of victims arrived from various quarters, without the cost of purchase, to supply their place.'

Litton Mill was probably the worst in England. It was remote from any town and the owner was the sort of person who seems to enjoy cruelty. The apprentices were very brutally treated, beaten and whipped for minor offences, and often punched or kicked by the overseers, not for doing anything wrong, but just 'for fun'. They were clothed in rags and were always dirty. 'The eldest girls had to comb and wash the younger apprentices—an irksome task, which was carelessly and partially performed. No soap was allowed—a small quantity of meal was given as a substitute, and this from the effects of keen hunger, was generally eaten.' Their usual food was 'rusty, half-*putrid*, fish-fed bacon and unpared turnips'. These were boiled in water and served for dinner. A few handfuls of meal were stirred into the greasy broth left over, and this was their supper.

Hungry factory children

Robert, now entering his teens, and not working under constant supervision, found a way of adding to his ration. Ellis Needham kept pigs to supply himself with pork and bacon, and these were given meal-balls, like dumplings, once a day: 'Blincoe and others, who worked in a part of the Mill whence they could see the swine served, used to say to one another—"The pigs are served; it will be our turn next." As soon as he saw the swineherd withdraw, he used to slip downstairs, and, stealing slyly towards the trough, plunge his hand in at the loopholes, and steal as many dumplings as he could.'

After some time, however, the pigs used to set up such a squealing when they saw the boys coming that the swineherd would come running up with his whip and chase them back to work.

At last in 1813, Robert's apprenticeship came to an end, as he was then twenty-one years old. When he left Litton Mill, he heard for the first time of an Act which Parliament had passed in 1802. This Act, called the Health and Morals of Apprentices Act, laid down certain rules about the training and care of factory apprentices, and gave Justices of the Peace the authority to inspect factories to see that the children were being properly treated.

The report of one such Magistrate, Mr H. H. Middleton, J.P., records the following, for the year 1810–11:
'LITTON MILL. Mr Ellis Needham. Clean.
'I found the house in which the Apprentices board, and lodge, very clean: but two of them having come to me with a complaint of being worked too hard, and of not having sufficient support, I thought it right to examine some of the Apprentices upon both, as to the facts they complained of, and the substance of their *deposition* is as follows; viz.
' "That they go into the Mill about ten minutes before six o'clock in the morning, and stay there till from ten to fifteen minutes after nine in the evening, excepting the time allowed for dinner, which is from half to three-quarters of an hour, that they have water-porridge for breakfast and supper and generally oatcake and treacle or oatcake and poor broth for dinner; that they are instructed in writing and reading on Sundays." '

Mr Middleton must have questioned the employer about the

poor food, because he goes on to report the following excuse: 'Mr John Needham said that the Mill was useless and the apprentices unemployed for a month in the winter in consequence of pulling down a water-wheel.'

Was one of the two who complained our Robert Blincoe? Notice that Mr Middleton did not ask any of the apprentices if they were treated well. They had to summon up courage to approach him, knowing that their employer would be violently angry when he heard of it.

Robert worked as a cotton-spinner for a few years after completing his apprenticeship, and, by saving every penny he could, managed to set himself up in business in Manchester in 1817 as a dealer in cotton-waste. He was lucky; lucky to escape the serious illnesses which killed others, lucky to avoid crippling accidents with the machines, lucky to survive the starvation diet and the brutal beatings.

Litton Mill was notoriously bad, of course. Few apprentices had quite such inhuman employers as Ellis Needham, and some were treated probably much better than in their original parish workhouse. Of the mill at Mellor, Mr Middleton wrote: 'Any *commendation* of mine must fall short of Mr Oldknow's very *meritorious* conduct towards the apprentices under his care, whose comfort in every respect seems to be his study: they were all looking very well and extremely clean.' (Samuel Oldknow was another of Richard Arkwright's many partners.)

At Cressbrook Mill, which stands only a mile or so down the valley of the Wye from Litton, Mr Middleton found that the apprentices worked from 6 a.m. to 8 p.m. with an hour off for dinner: 'Their diet consists of milk, or milk-porridge, for breakfast and supper, and they have flesh meat every day at dinner. They looked well and appeared perfectly satisfied with their situation.'

Most of the mills like Lowdham, Litton and Cressbrook, which used parish apprentices, were built far away from any town. They were built on a site where the water-power was available but where workers were not. And so the workers had to be brought to the mill. There were other mills which were built in or near a small town or a group of villages. In these, it was not necessary to bring

Cressbrook Mill

parish apprentices hundreds of miles to work. The local people, and their children, could be got to work, provided they wanted to. First they had to be told that jobs were being offered. Jedediah Strutt in Belper and Richard Arkwright at Cromford advertised for workers in the 'Derby Mercury'. Let us take a look at one of Arkwright's notices:

'WANTED

'At Cromford, in the County of Derby, Forging and Filing Smiths, Joiners and Carpenters, Framework-Knitters and Weavers, with large Families. Likewise Children of all Ages; above seven Years old, may have constant Employment. Boys and young Men may have Trades taught them, which will enable them to maintain a Family in a short Time. Two or three young Men who can write a good Hand, are also wanted.

'By personal application at the COTTON-MILLS Particulars may be known.'

You have seen in the first chapter how people with a large number of children often found it difficult to make ends meet. 39

Here was an employer actually asking for people with large families and promising jobs for the children! Notice the emphasis on 'constant employment'. Why do you think a cotton-mill would require some young men who could write neatly?

The children of Belper were ready in 1776 to respond to this sort of offer, perhaps with a little persuasion from their parents. Young men and women from the surrounding villages were also taken on, some of them walking three or four miles into the mills to work and the same distance home again in the evening. Whole families moved into Belper, if they could find a place to live. We can imagine the Ward family whom we described in chapter One moving to Belper to work for the Strutts. Sam Ward and Jacob might be employed in the mill workshops, making and repairing iron nails, bolts, brackets and fittings of all kinds. Martha, the mother of the family, would now have all the house-keeping to do herself, and be fully occupied with that and looking after Mary. Margaret, Isaac and Dick could all earn a regular weekly wage in the mill.

How much would they earn in a week? It depended on how much work they could do. Like the domestic workers, their wages were calculated on the amount of work which they com-pleted, and ranged from 4s downwards. Overseers were paid more; between 6s and 10s a week. For these wages, they worked twelve hours a day, six days a week. They began at six o'clock in the morning, and worked until mid-day, when they had an hour off for dinner. At one o'clock, they began again and went on until seven in the evening. During the morning they had a fifteen-minute break, and another in the afternoon. They could have a bite to eat then, if they had brought anything with them. In the early nineteenth century, the workers could get a pint of tea or coffee at each break by paying one penny a day.

What sort of work did they do? Most mill children were piecers. They had to tie or 'piece' together any threads which broke on the spinning machines. William Hutton, a mill apprentice, wrote: 'The workman's care is chiefly to unite, by a knot, a thread that breaks; to take out the burs and uneven parts. The threads are continually breaking, and to tye them is prin-cipally the business of children whose fingers are nimble.' This meant walking up and down in front of the frames. 'One person commands from 20-60 threads. If many cease, at the same time, to turn, it amounts to a fault, and is succeeded by punishment.'

Each child working on the spinning frames had to see that the machine was properly oiled and regularly cleaned. If any oil or grease got on the yarn it would be spoiled. Some children had to collect the full bobbins or reels in small trucks, and take them to be checked and counted. Others went round giving out empty reels and cotton to be spun. Children also worked at cleaning the raw cotton. When a bale had been opened and inspected, they had to pick it over by hand, and take out any twigs, bits of leaf, or other rubbish. The older boys could do heavier work – unloading bales of cotton, and making up the parcels of yarn for delivery.

Unlike the domestic workers, they were under constant supervision, and could not work as and when they pleased. In order to keep a check on slackness and misbehaviour, the Strutts did not pay their employees their full wages at the end of each week. One-sixth was kept back, and paid as a kind of bonus every three months. Fines for breaking rules or for being absent without permission were deducted from this Quarterly Gift Money, and for serious offences the whole amount was sometimes withheld.

The amounts of the fines are not always given in the account books but here is a list of some of the offences. Remember the workers were mostly children, teenagers, and young men and women:

Staying off without leave.
Going to Derby Fair.
Being off drinking.
Stealing pack-thread.
Stealing Candles, Oil, &c.
Making waste of good yarn.
Neglecting cleaning and oiling.
Tying bad knots.

There was also a good deal of horseplay and fighting among the younger workers. A well run mill could not permit this sort of conduct:

Riding on each other's back.

Striking T. Ride on the nose.
Throwing tea on Josh Bridworth.
Using ill language.
Throwing Water on Ann Gregory very frequently.

The Strutts were firm believers in orderly behaviour, and also used fines as a punishment for offences committed outside working hours. Any excess of youthful high spirits on the part of a mill worker might mean a deduction from his or her wages.

These are some of the things for which fines were imposed: Receiving potatoes of Martha Booth which she had stolen from home. For putting Josh Haynes' dog into a bucket of Hot water. Rubbing their faces with blood and going about the town to frighten people.

A worker who avoided such faults got full wages. Many workers, however, had voluntary deductions made in their wages, for rent and goods.

The building of houses for workers began under Jedediah and continued after his death. If the Strutt firm wanted people to come to Belper to work for them then housing must be provided— good houses at reasonable rents. Two long rows of houses were

Long Row, Belper

begun at Belper in the 1790s. These are simply called Long Row, and are conveniently near the mills, as you can see from the map. A little way beyond these were built the Clusters. These were blocks of four houses, and seem to have been intended for overseers. At the same time, about sixty houses were built at Milford also.

Let's have a look at one of these mill houses, in Long Row. The front door opens into a living-room which is about thirteen feet square. There is one window and a fireplace. In one corner there is a small larder. At the back of the house is a small kitchen, and a coal-store just inside the back door. Upstairs, on each of the two upper floors is a large bedroom. The lavatory is a separate little building in the back garden. The whole house is strongly built of stone, has a stone floor, and is roofed with good slate.

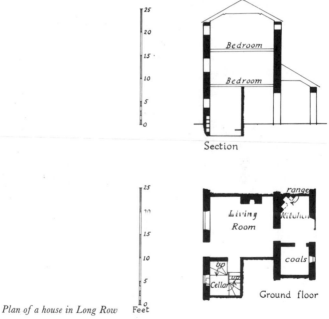

Section

Plan of a house in Long Row   Feet

Ground floor

The Strutts kept a check on their tenants to see that they were treating the house properly. They were whitewashed inside every year, and the chimneys were swept every quarter.

43

A writer in 1813 declared that this kind of house set a good example to landlords elsewhere:

'The vast numbers of neat and comfortable Cottages which have been erected, by the late Sir Richard, and by the present Mr Richard Arkwright, by Messrs. Strutts, Mr Samuel Oldknow, and numerous others of the Cotton-spinners and Manufacturers, for the accommodation of their multitudes of workpeople, must have had a great influence on the general style and condition, now observable in the Cottages.'

And he goes on to say: 'Their Rents are in general moderate, and adapted to the earnings and conditions of the Occupants.' The rents which the Strutts charged were about two or three shillings a week. One child in a family could earn at least enough to pay the rent.

A neat house at a reasonable rent was not the only benefit to go with working in the mills. Jedediah Strutt and his sons were careful that the families they employed should have adequate food. As the town grew rapidly with the expansion of cotton-spinning, the butchers, grocers and other shops of the town were unable to keep pace with the demand. There was also the danger that shopkeepers would take advantage of the people's needs to put food prices up.

Mill-workers bought meat and bacon, dripping, potatoes and a variety of vegetables and fruit from the mill. An account was kept, and the amount was deducted from the weekly wage.

Another advantage of working in the cotton-mills in Belper was that children could get free schooling.

In August 1785 the 'Derby Mercury' reported:

'We hear from Belper that Mr Strutt has, (with a Liberality which does Honour to the human Heart) entirely at his own Expense, instituted a SUNDAY SCHOOL for the Benefit of All the Youth of both Sexes employed in his Cotton Mill at that Town; and provides them with all necessary Books &c. for learning to read and write. This school was opened on July 3, and 120 Scholars have already been admitted.—An Example worthy of Imitation by all whom *Providence* has blessed with *Affluence*.'

Many mill owners, however, did not follow Strutt's example, either in providing housing, food, or education. The owners of factories which were built in towns usually left their employees to fend for themselves. Some factory owners even kept a shop at which their workers were compelled to spend some of their wages each week, and the quality of the goods was not always the best! In many mills, the overseers used a whip or a strap as punishment for the children, and if the parents complained the children lost their jobs.

Although the young people in the Belper mills might find twelve hours' work a day six days a week, and school on Sunday rather unpleasant, there were others who were worse off, and many had been worse off before the mills were built. Now, if they were working in the mills, they had regular work and regular wages, satisfying food, the chance of a good house to live in, and the opportunity to get an education.

Building houses for mill-hands

4 The New Community

The employees of Messrs. Strutts were not the only people who were helped by the building of the cotton mills in Belper and Milford. The village grew rapidly into a town and the whole community changed.

There were 532 inhabitants in 1741. William Pilkington, who visited Belper in 1789, wrote:

'Every year, almost every month, new houses are rising up. This rapid increase in the state of population is chiefly owing to the erection of two large cotton mills in the village by Mr Strutt. These machines alone, afford employment to about six hundred hands, principally women, and children.'

Britton and Brayley who wrote a book in 1802 called 'The Beauties of England and Wales' described Belper as 'one of the most flourishing places in Derbyshire; it appearing by the returns made under the late act for numbering the people, that its population *exceeds* that of every town in the county, excepting Derby; though some years ago it was but an *inconsiderable* village'.

The Act referred to was the Act of Parliament which established the first official Census, in 1801. There were, in fact, 4,509 people there then. Ten years later, when another Census was taken, the population had again increased, to 5,773. In 1821 there were over 7,000 and by 1831 there were 9,000.

The changes were not merely an adding of new houses and more families. As well as growing in size, Belper grew in what was then called civility. This was very greatly as a result of the ideas, the example and the action of the Strutt family.

One of the things which the cotton mills needed was a better system of transport and communication. Think of it. The raw cotton had to be brought to the mills at Belper and Milford. The

Cargo at the docks

spun yarn had to be sent off to the hosiers in Nottingham, the weavers of Lancashire, and other customers. Suppose that a dealer needs an extra supply of yarn quickly. Can Strutts supply it? He must write to them and it will take several days to get an answer back. Suppose that an important customer does not receive a delivery of yarn which he is expecting. He must write to Strutts to find out why there has been a delay. Suppose that a shipment of raw cotton arrives at the mills in bad condition. They must write to the shippers to complain and arrange for a reduction in the price. Remember that there was no telephone or telegraph.

The Strutts could not get and send off regular waggon-loads of cotton on the roads as they were before 1776. You have read how William Blount thought nothing of digging up the King's Highway to get coal in 1748. Although the Derbyshire J.P.s in the Court of Quarter Sessions knew that Belper's roads were bad, they usually put off doing anything about them. In 1732, for example, the Court record reads: 'Ordered by this Court that all process against the Inhabitants of Belper in this County touching the irrepair of their Highways be *respited* till next Sessions.'

In 1747 the J.P.s went so far as to order Duffield to repair their road to Derby, which, they recorded 'was and yet is in a very ruinous, miry, deep, broken condition'.

Strutt's mills simply could not do their business on such roads. So the firm began to build roads at their own expense. The road from Milford to Belper was so much improved that it amounted to rebuilding. The ford which gave the place its name was replaced by a stone bridge in 1790 'a handsome, solid structure, remarkable for its neatness', and the firm also built a footbridge supported by chains, for pedestrians. In 1817, John Farey the surveyor, noted: 'A good road exists at present up the Vale of the Derwent, from Duffield to Belper-bridge' and he suggested that:

'It would be very important to the public, that a good Road should be made up the West side of the River to Cromford, nearly along the line of a private Carriage-way between those places, belonging to Messrs. Strutts, Charles Hurt, and Richard Arkwright, Esqrs. whose public spirit and liberal views, would, I think, induce them readily to *concur* in making this public Road.'

In fact, the new public road was built along the east side of the river. It was already being built before Farey's suggestion was put into print. In July 1817 a meeting of trustees was held at the Greyhound Inn at Cromford to consider *tenders* for building *toll-houses:* 'and also for the purpose of letting the forming and making such of the lengths of the said Road which have not already been taken.'

The Swann Inn, Nottingham

Cromford was already connected to Manchester and the North, Belper was linked by road to Derby and thence to London and the South. When the new road between Cromford and Belper was opened in 1820 it was the final link in an additional North-South route. Nowadays the Milford-Belper-Cromford road forms part of the A6 trunk road. Stephen Glover writing about Belper in 1829 remarked on the new line of road and the traffic on it: 'Post coaches from London and Manchester, Birmingham and Shef- field, and Nottingham and Manchester pass through, to and from those towns, daily.'

The 'Telegraph' coach called at the Red Lion every day at one o'clock, on its journey from Sheffield to Birmingham, and passed through on its return journey at four o'clock. The 'Lord Nelson' from Nottingham stopped at the Red Lion at 9 a.m. and returned from Manchester at half-past one. The 'Peveril of the Peak' from London to Manchester also passed through Belper every day at one o'clock. What a fine sight, to stand by the mills between one and half-past and see the three great stage-coaches 49

A mail coach

bowling along, the paint shining, the brasswork gleaming, the horses' hooves striking sparks from the road!

The Strutts were most interested in the main river-valley route, because it was along this that their cotton was brought and their yarn sent away. As Belper grew, however, there were so many more people and so much more traffic that it became worthwhile to adopt the turnpike system. This meant collecting a small sum of money called a *toll* from all who used a certain road. The right to collect the tolls was often sold by auction. Here is a notice announcing such an auction:

BELPER ROAD

TOLLS TO BE LET

Notice is hereby Given that a Meeting of the Trustees appointed in and by virtue of the Acts of Parliament passed in the 33rd and 54th years of the Reign of his present Majesty King George The Third, for repairing, widening, altering and improving the Road from Heage, in the County of Derby, through Belper to Duffield, in the said County, will be held at the House of George Henn, known by the Sign of the White Hart, in Duffield aforesaid, on Monday, the Thirteenth day of October next, at Two o'clock in the Afternoon; and that at the same Time and place, the Tolls arising at the several Toll Gates and Chain upon the said Turnpike Road, called or known by the several Names of the Laund Side Gate, Crich Road Chain, and Millford Bridge Gate and Side Gate, will be offered to be

Let by Auction

To the best Bidder, for the term of one year commencing at Twelve at Noon of the Eighth day of November next . . .

which Tolls are let this present year for the clear Sum of Five Hundred and Twelve Pounds, and will be put up at that Sum.

Robert Evans.

Clerk to the Trustees.

Can you find out which years were the 33rd and 54th of George III? You will notice that the first was not long after the building of Milford Bridge. The person bidding for the right to collect the tolls would have to be prepared to pay at least £512 and perhaps more, but he would expect to collect much more than that in tolls the following year, and so make a profit for himself. Can you work out how many horsemen at a penny a time or how many carts or carriages at sixpence would pass the four toll gates to bring in £512 in a year?

Along the 'repaired, widened, altered and improved' roads came a postal service, vital to the mills but also useful to everyone who lived in Belper. Up to 1792 the nearest postal service was at Wirksworth, miles away. From there a post-boy on horseback carried the mail to Derby direct. With the growth of Belper from 1776 onwards there was a demand for a postal collection in the town. The Lord of the Manor of Belper, Paul Joddrell, put forward his own bailiff, Samuel Taylor, as 'Receiver' and announced that he would charge an extra penny on every letter handed in. This caused an outcry among the people of Belper. Apart from the extra charge above the normal cost of postage, Samuel Taylor's house was in a field half a mile away from any road, so people would have to go right outside the town to hand in, or post, their letters.

A meeting of some of the leading citizens was held on 23 December 1793, to draw up a report to be sent to the Postmaster-General.

The report was signed by forty-four people, including G. B. Strutt and Abraham Harrison, the nailmaster. Strutt was one of those appointed to hand the report to the Postmaster-General. On reading it, the Postmaster-General made the note: 'Mr Joddrell does not seem to have one foot of ground to stand on.'

A Receiver was appointed who lived in the town itself, and Strutts made an arrangement by which the mail-rider called at the mills to collect a private bag of mail instead of its being handed in to the Receiver.

If you know something about changes in transport in the eighteenth century, you might expect that a rising cotton town would have a canal. Many canals were built between about 1760 and 1830 to serve industrial areas. Richard Arkwright built a canal to link Cromford with Nottingham in 1792 and a branch cut from Ambergate on the Cromford Canal to Belper was being considered in 1801. This plan was never carried out. There was a good road to Derby and a canal begun in 1793, linking Derby with the Trent, provided cheap water transport to Nottingham.

Looking forward, in 1839, George Stephenson building the Derby to Leeds section of the Midland Railway, took the line through Belper. This meant that the mills, and the people, were then brought into the national network of railways covering the whole country.

The better roads and the establishment of a postal service in the 1790s and early 1800s were mainly brought about by the presence of the cotton mills. The fact that good transport and communication existed also made it easier for other industries to expand. You might think that the establishment of the cotton industry in Belper would lead to a decline in the original nailmaking. People living at the time seemed to think so.

A post boy

Pilkington, writing in 1789, considered that nailmaking employed about 200 people but was declining. Glover, recorded in 1829, that the manufacture of nails still supported 300-400 hands but was 'thought to be declining'. In fact, the increase in the population meant a much greater local demand for nails, for building and for horse-shoes, while the improved roads meant that the nailmasters could sell them farther afield. In 1825, John Harrison the nailmaster was writing to his son, Thomas, at the White Bear Inn, Basinghall Street, London:

'I am not certain but I think you had not the name of Messrs Vardon & Lea, No. — Grace Church St in your list. I believe Messrs. White & Co., 346 Oxf^d St has not had the *Invoice* of those you have account of, but we have been packing the remainder of their order and I will send them the Invoice either this morn^g or on Sunday morn^g all together. If you have not wrote when you receive this dont fail writing by the first post, but there will be no mail out of London from Saturday night until Monday night. Take care to examine your bedroom every night that there is nobody under the bed or in the room.'

Orders of nails were being sent by road-waggon to wholesale merchants as far away as London. Letters and invoices could be sent by reliable post, but London was still regarded as a dangerous place for crime as we see from that final warning!

The nailmaking industry expanded but did not otherwise change. It continued to be run under the domestic system. The

53

habit of keeping St Monday amongst the nailers went on and, like many workers who remained in domestic industries, they became worse-off than their neighbours who were in factory work. Farey noticed in 1817 that it was possible for a good nailer to earn 'a shilling or more an hour; notwithstanding which, the Families of the Nailers appeared to me, very poor and distressed, when compared with the Cotton and other Manufacturing Families of the place'. Nailmaking by hand did not completely die out until the early twentieth century. In 1901 there were still thirty-eight nailers in Belper.

Framework-knitting continued in Belper also, and it also grew in importance. Belper became one of the secondary centres after Derby and Nottingham, with its own hosiers, putting-out work to people in the town itself and in neighbouring hamlets. The largest hosiers with their own warehouse and office in Belper were Messrs Ward, Brettle and Ward, who, in 1829, according to Glover 'employ about four hundred silk-stocking frames and 2,500 cotton-hose-frames'. The present knitwear factory of Messrs Brettles in Belper was built in 1834 as a putting-out warehouse and the last domestic framework-knitter was still working on his own frame at home in Bargate, near Belper, until 1913.

You have already seen that the children employed in the mills had been able to attend a Sunday School as early as 1785. By 1815 there were other schools, both day schools and Sunday schools, which any child could attend. The most that any of these charged in fees was one penny per week, and some were free. In a Sunday School, of course, the pupils were taught reading, writing and arithmetic, as in a day school. It was simply a school held on Sunday because that was the only day that most children would be free to go to school. These had been founded by people following the example of the Strutts. They were all run by some church or chapel in the town.

When the first mill was built in 1776, the only place of worship was the little Anglican chapel of St John near the Market Place, which had been built in the twelfth century. There was no resident clergyman. The vicar of Duffield held a service in Belper on alternate Sundays and that was all. Private

A schoolroom

houses were licensed from time to time for Protestant *Dissenters* to meet in and worship.

The Strutt family were *Unitarians* and Jedediah himself built a Chapel in Field Row in 1782. By 1820, there were Congregationalist, Baptist, Wesleyan and Primitive Methodist chapels in the town. The Strutts encouraged and helped any religious group in the belief that belonging to a church produced better citizens and more reliable workers. William Clowes, a leader of the Primitive Methodists, wrote about a preaching campaign in Belper in 1814:

'Mr. Strutt, the proprietor of several cotton factories, perceiving a decided change in many of his workpeople *wrought* by our *instrumentality*, became very friendly to us. The place in which we worshipped becoming too small, we applied to him for land on which to build a chapel, when he kindly offered us as much land as we wanted at one shilling a yard. A chapel was soon built which I and others had the pleasure to open.'

In 1822 the Church of England, rather late perhaps, but on a grander scale than the Nonconformist groups, began the building of a new parish church, St Peter's. On 31 October, the foundation stone was laid by the Duke of Devonshire. An eyewitness described the scene like this:

'On the 31st October, 1822, the first stone of a new church was laid, amid an immense *concourse* of people. It was on the day of a great annual fair, and the day was uncommonly fine. The Duke of Devonshire, who had announced his intention to *officiate* at the ceremony of laying the first stone was met by the delighted multitude at an early hour: his travelling *equipage* was stopped by the crowd, the horses were taken from the carriage, and his Grace was drawn by the shouting populace to Bridge Hill, the residence of G. B. Strutt, esq. where he breakfasted.'

After the ceremony: 'His Grace returned in state to Bridge Hill, accompanied by a large *cavalcade* of his *tenantry,* and honoured Mr & Mrs G. B. Strutt by dining and remaining all night at their house.'

Excellent turnpike roads, a regular postal service, a general air of expansion and prosperity, schools, new churches—these were some of the things which followed the building of the cotton mills in Belper and which helped to create a new community.

A writer in 1829, referring to the town holiday or 'wakes' in July, stated: 'The disgraceful sports of bull-baiting, badger and bear-baiting, cock-fighting and throwing, which were formerly very common at these wakes, are now falling into disuse. Cocking and dog-fighting continue, we regret to say, to be too much practised.'

The influence of the Strutts, which affected the whole community, was totally against such barbarous sports. Although the owners of the mills were constantly trying to create habits of regularity, hard work and respectability among their employees and throughout the community, they were willing, on suitable occasions, to take a lead in town festivities.

In 1814, when Napoleon was defeated, a holiday was declared:

'REJOICINGS AT BELPER AND MILLFORD

'Friday *se'nnight* at 9 o'clock in the forenoon, a discharge of cannon summoned the numerous people employed in Messrs Strutt's manufactory at Belper to meet at the mills, from whence they marched in regular procession, round the town, preceded by banners with appropriate devices, mottos and an excellent band playing the most loyal and popular airs.'

In the mills a large room was prepared for a feast:

'The dining room was decorated with great taste and elegance. On the one end over the head of the table were 'G.R. Peace P.R.' in large letters composed of gilt and plain laurel leaves and ribbons; the other end over a long range of barrels of ale, the word 'Plenty' was very *appositely* placed, and on the end of one wing along which four tables extended, appeared the immortal name of "Wellington".

'After the company had sufficiently paid their *devoirs* to the ale barrels, they adjourned to the dancing room which was decorated with equal taste, and after the dancing was concluded, a display of fire-works terminated an entertainment which neither the participators, or spectators, can ever see surpassed.'

The children of the town marched in a separate parade:

'At 9 o'clock 1300 children assembled, who paraded the town headed by the gentlemen of the Derby Cavalry Band. The children were each regaled with a two-penny bun and ale. Two oxen and five sheep were roasted whole and distributed among six hundred and fifty families, together with a loaf and quart of ale each.'

A great novelty for the occasion was the release of a balloon.

'At one o'clock a discharge of cannon in the market place announced the ascent of a balloon of large *dimensions,* made by Mr Harrison, from which a beautiful car was suspended, which went off in grand stile amidst the acclamations of thousands of spectators, and continued in sight nearly nine minutes.—The clean and decent appearance of the people in Mr Strutt's procession, and the children of the town was highly creditable to themselves and gratifying to the spectators.'

5 Hard Times

These festivities under the benevolent but watchful eye of Messrs Strutts were modelled on the entertainments provided by Arkwright at the original mill at Cromford.

In September 1776 the 'Derby Mercury' reported:

'We hear from Cromford in this County, that on Monday last, (being the Wakes there, as well as the Candle-lighting at the Cotton-Mills of Messrs. Arkwright, and Co.) a grand Procession was made from the Mills round the Town, by the Workmen, Children &c., in Number about 500; they were preceded by a Band of Music, next to whom followed a Boy working in a Weaver's Loom, drawn by a white Horse; in this Manner they returned (through an amazing Concourse of People, who express'd their Satisfaction by the loudest *Plaudits*) to the Mills, where they were plentifully supplied with Buns and Ale, Nuts, Fruit &c., and the evening concluded with Music and Dancing.—The same Day a Feast or Rearing Dinner, was given to upwards of 200 Workmen &c. who have this Summer erected another large Cotton Mill, which is 120 Feet in length, and seven Stories high. Notwithstanding they were regaled with a large Quantity of Strong Beer &c. yet the Day was spent with the greatest Harmony imaginable.'

The mill which the Rearing Dinner was given for was the second at Cromford, while Arkwright was still in partnership with Strutt. The first Belper mill, you may remember, was built the same year. Satisfaction and harmony it would seem followed cotton mills everywhere they were built. Yet only three years later, the newspapers in Manchester and Derby printed the following letter 'written from Cromford to a Gentleman in Manchester':

'In your last you expressed some Fear of the Mob coming to Destroy the Works at Cromford, but they are well prepared to receive them should they come there. All the Gentlemen in this Neighbourhood being determined to support Mr Arkwright, in defence of his Works, which have been of such *Utility* to this Country, Fifteen hundred Stand of small Arms are already collected from Derby and the Neighbouring Towns, and great Battery of Cannon raised of 9 and 12 Pounders with great plenty of Powder and Grape Shot, besides which, upwards of 500 Spears are fixt in Poles of between 2 and 3 yards long. The Spears and Battery are always to be kept in Repair for the Defence of the Works and Protection of the Village, and 5 or 6,000 Men, Miners, &c. can at any Time be assembled in less than an Hour, by Signals agreed upon, who are determined to defend to the very last Extremity, the Works, by which many Hundreds of their Wives and Children get a decent and comfortable Livelihood.'

Quite a contrast from buns, ale and music to guns, spears and cannon! Though the amount of the armaments may be exaggerated in order to deter the possible attack there was no doubt that the people of Cromford were prepared to defend the mills.

Who was coming to destroy the works? Where were they coming from? and why? The mob were hand-spinners from Lancashire, where they had recently attacked ten factories, including one of Arkwright's mills at Birkacre, near Chorley. So it seemed possible, in spite of the distance, that they might come to Cromford. In fact, they never came. But why were people trying to burn down spinning mills and destroy the machines?

Notice that the men who were preparing to defend the works were miners—lead miners—and their reason was that the cotton mills provided work for their wives and children. The position was much the same as in Belper, where the mills provided extra employment for the nailers' families without taking work from the nailers themselves! But the mob was from Lancashire where men were already working in their homes spinning and where mills employing women and children 59 were in competition with the hand-spinners. The machines produced yarn much faster and cheaper, and the domestic spinners found it difficult or impossible to live on the wages they got because the amount of yarn they could spin at home was so much less than could be spun by machine. Many became unemployed or could earn only a few shillings a week. As their work dwindled they turned their full anger against the new mills.

Unfortunately, hardship was not only caused by machines putting men out of work. Throughout the eighteenth century, the enclosure of village commons and open fields was going on, which meant that many poor people, losing their common rights, found it even more difficult to make a living. You can read about enclosure and its effects in the book in this series called 'The Agrarian Revolution'.

One of the things which accompanied enclosure was that landlords made harsher rules against poachers.

In 1813, the Lord of the Manor of Belper issued the following warning in the 'Derbyshire Chronicle':

GAME

Whereas the GAME in the Manor and Liberty of BELPER has been much destroyed by Poachers and unqualified Persons

NOTICE IS HEREBY GIVEN

That Men are employed to Watch and detect those found with Dogs, Guns, &c; and every Person so found, after this Notice, will be proceeded against according to Law.

J. F. Williamson, pro R. P. Jodrell, Esq. N.B. Any Person found out of the Paths in the Lands, Woods and Plantations (on any Pretence) belonging to R. P. Jodrell, Esq. in this Liberty, will be prosecuted.

Belper, Dec. 4, 1813.

Poaching became more widespread because the increasing cost of food made it harder for poor people to make an honest living. Food prices went up because of the difficulty of importing corn during the wars with France.

A poacher caught

In 1789 the great revolution began in France during which the common people overthrew the French King and smashed the power of the nobles. Some people in England approved of what the revolutionary leaders were doing. Others disliked the revolution, thinking it was too violent and bloodthirsty. The British Government and Parliament elected by the landowners became afraid that the poor people in Britain would copy the French and try to gain more power for themselves. When war broke out between Britain and France in 1793 the fear of revolt made the Government and wealthy people generally believe that the lower classes must be kept down at all costs. Any sign of organised action by the working class was looked on as the first step towards a revolution and the smallest offence against the law was punished with the utmost severity. This was all the more unfortunate because the war sent the price of food soaring, and by hampering the export of goods caused employers to lay off or dismiss large numbers of their workers. So the people in many parts of England had good reason to protest about rising prices, low wages, and unemployment, just at the time when the authorities were

E

in no mood to listen to such protests.

The wars lasted from 1793 to 1815 but even afterwards for some years there was a great deal of distress among the workers.

Poaching, ordinary stealing and illegal meetings of workmen all made the people in authority very anxious, because there was no police force to deal with crime. Unpaid, spare-time village constables and town watchmen were usually over-worked and outnumbered. During these troubled years from the 1790s to the 1820s, the better-off people in many places tried to reduce crime by forming their own voluntary associations which offered rewards to anyone who would report criminal activities.

In Belper, the Association was founded early in 1793, with thirty-nine members.

This Association was intended to deal with ordinary crime. Another, called the Loyal Association, was formed to prevent and report to the authorities any revolutionary ideas—such as the demand that more people should have the right to vote.

Belper escaped riots and serious crime but the satisfied, thriving and law-abiding citizens could read of troubles not very far away, in and around Nottingham.

Here is an account of one incident which occurred in the neighbourhood of Nottingham in July 1814. It concerns the smashing of four stocking-frames by a gang of men. The frames were rented by Mr Hooton of the village of Sneinton:

'When they were heard, about half-past twelve o'clock, opening the little garden gate before the house, Hooton and his wife jumped out of bed; and throwing open a window, saw about twelve men (it is supposed there were many more stationed round the house) advancing towards them. Being immediately struck with the character and object of their visitors, they exclaimed, "For God's sake, what do you mean to do?" on which they were ordered with bitter *imprecations* to put in their heads immediately, or have their brains blown out. They accordingly left the window; but called out "Murder! Murder!" as loud as possible in their bedroom.

'A shot was then discharged and a large stone thrown at them, which obliged them to go to other parts of the house where they made noise enough to alarm their neighbours, who, however, dared not go to their assistance.'

The gang broke open the door and held Hooton and his wife prisoner in their bedroom while they smashed up the frames. Some of them wounded a pig belonging to Hooton and tried to chop down his apple tree.

They then went on to New Sneinton where they broke another frame, and rounded off their night's work by destroying two more frames in a house in Trumpet Street in Nottingham itself.

Men who went about smashing stocking-frames or machines in mills were called Luddites. They were supposed to have a leader named Ned Ludd, although in fact no over-all leader existed. The chief of each gang which was got together used the name Ned Ludd or 'General Ludd' in order to conceal his true name.

The Luddite gangs broke frames belonging to hosiers who paid low wages, and sometimes larger-than-usual frames which they believed would cause unemployment by enabling the work to be done quicker.

Luddite action had started in March 1811, when the trade was slack, many framework-knitters were out of work, wages were cut by the hosiers and food prices were high. Troops were sent in to Nottingham by the authorities, 800 horse-soldiers, and 1,000 infantry. A 10 p.m. curfew was imposed and in desperation Parliament passed an Act making frame-breaking a crime punishable by death. These measures brought this outbreak of Luddism to an end, but they did not make the stockingers any better off, and when the death penalty for frame-breaking was removed after about a year, Luddism began again. The lives of the stockingers and of the small shopkeepers who depended on their custom varied from grim to desperate. In the autumn of 1816, in the Nottinghamshire parish of Hinckley, of 1200 families 600 were out of work, 300 were so poor that they were excused from paying the Poor Rate, so the remaining 300 families were expected to contribute enough to support all the rest. You can imagine that did not leave them with much to spend beyond bare necessities.

Luddites in action

Poverty, high food prices, unemployment, and the use of troops to prevent riots and disorder kept Nottingham and many other places in a state of alarm throughout 1816 and on into the year 1817. Then in June 1817, there came what the government thought was the beginning of the expected revolution of the cotton and woollen workers of the Midlands. The 'Revolution' was centered on Pentrich, about five miles from Belper. The 'Derby Mercury' broke the news to its readers with suitable gravity. It blamed those people who had for so many years been trying 'to excite a spirit of discontent and *sedition*, in the lower classes of people throughout the kingdom'.

These were members of the group of Radicals, or reformers who, amongst other things, wanted more people to have the right to vote. The lower classes, in fact, would have preferred cheaper bread. The Corn Law passed in 1815 was keeping the price of bread at its high wartime level.

What happened, then, in this Pentrich Revolution? Word was spread among the poor along the Derbyshire-Nottingham-shire border, in June 1817, that 'Monday, the 9th instant was fixed for a general *insurrection* in Lancashire, Yorkshire, Derby-shire and Nottinghamshire and that immense bodies of men armed with guns, *pikes* and other offensive weapons were to have marched into the town of Nottingham'.

The plan was then to set up a provisional government to link up with those in the other areas:

'Under this *delusion* a party of about fifty or sixty men from the village and neighbourhood of South Wingfield, under the command of a leader deputed from the town of Nottingham, armed with pikes and some guns, assembled about 12 o'clock in the night of Monday the 9th inst. in Wingfield Park.

'At the same hour a party of *insurgents* assembled in the adjoining village of Pentridge, the seat of the conspiracy.'

The gangs joined forces and during the early morning marched through Ripley, to the top of Codnor Common. Small groups of men from neighbouring places joined them, many under threat of being killed or beaten up if they refused. One man, but only one was, in fact, shot dead, for refusing either to join the march or give up a gun which he had. Many better-off people were compelled to supply guns or money to the marchers.

It is worth noticing that they marched through the iron works of Jessop and Company at Butterley. Jessop was a considerate employer who treated his employees well. Very few of his men could be persuaded to join in the march.

When they got to Codnor Common there was an inn, and the temptation was too much to resist:

'The insurgents remained nearly an hour at the public house at the northwardly end of Codnor Common, probably in the expectation of further reinforcements and dispatches from the town of Nottingham. Here, notwithstanding the refreshments which were given to them by their commander, their spirits became evidently depressed.'

A labourer

There were now about 300 of them. At about 6 o'clock in the morning they set off again on the road to Nottingham. It was not long before the expected messenger arrived from Nottingham, with the news that the troops there had mutinied and refused to march against them. This was untrue, and most of the men did not believe it. In the clear morning light it was harder for them to have the same confidence as they had under cover of darkness. The end of the 'Revolution' was not far away:

'The Commander quitted the rear of the party and took the lead of it; he quickened his march; and became regardless of the desertions which took place at every crossroad and corner. However, they proceeded as far as Kimberley, at which place their numbers were reduced to fifty—here they were met and immediately *repulsed* by a party of Hussars under the command of Captain Phillipps from Nottingham. Several prisoners and a

An Officer of Hussars

considerable number of pikes, guns, pitch-forks and other offensive weapons were taken and carried under an escort of the Hussars into Nottingham.'

Those who were captured on the road or rounded up and arrested later were put on trial, unless they were able to prove that they had been forced into joining the march against their will. They were put on trial for high treason—that is, attempting to harm the King and to overthrow the government by force. Such a thing was obviously impossible for a few hundred half-armed miners and stockingers, but it was enough that they should have intended to do so.

Did the marchers think that they could overthrow the government? Did they want to? One of them gave evidence as a witness at the trial. His name was Shirley Astbury. The leaders told him, he said 'that on getting a supply of arms the party should immediately proceed to Nottingham where each would receive 100 guineas with plenty of rum. After taking possession of Nottingham they were then to go down the Trent, but for what purpose witness did not understand.'

Do you think that many of the rebels had joined for the promised guineas and rum, and, like Astbury, had not troubled their minds with what was to happen after that?

Another witness had heard the commander, Jeremiah Brandreth, quote this verse to get men to join:

'Every man his skill must try;
He must turn out and not deny.
No Bloody Soldiers must we dread;
We must turn out and fight for bread.
The time is come you plain must see,
The Government opposed must be.'

Notice what it is the rhyme says they were to fight for. The leaders believed that they were to be just a part of a general uprising of the poor, the hungry, and the unemployed, but they had been told this by a man named Oliver, who had in fact been hired by the government to encourage such plots and then betray the plotters. Oliver had been in Pentrich some months earlier but had left as soon as he was sure the plot had been taken up by the people he had deceived.

You will probably think it hardly fair that men should be punished for being misled by a government spy, but the authorities took the view that they were wrong to have listened to such plots in the first place. They were determined that they should receive full punishment and everything was done to impress the people of Derbyshire and the whole of the Midlands with the sight of justice being enforced.

The trial of the prisoners began in Derby at the end of September 1817. Here is a description of the arrival in Derby of the High Sheriff for the county: 'Besides the full *retinue* of *javelin men* &c, he was accompanied by an attendance unusually numerous, which included the principal gentlemen and *yeomanry* of Alfreton and Ripley.'

The Sheriff and his following then went on to meet the two judges on the road from London, and returned with them in an impressive procession:

'At four o'clock their Lordships, the Judges, Abbott and Holroyd, were conducted into the town in the following order: the Special Constables, two and two, each bearing a light

Jeremiah Brandreth

wand to designate his office,—The Mayor (the Rev. C. S. Hope) on horseback,—the Sheriff's Men,—Gaoler and Sheriff's Bailiff,—The Under-Sheriff, all on horseback,—The Carriages of the Judges closed the procession.'

The next morning, twelve of the prisoners were brought to Derby under an escort of the 15th Light Dragoons and the trials began. A citizen of Belper, Thomas Wragg, was one of the solicitors for the forty-six prisoners. The prosecution concentrated on three who were looked on as the ringleaders, Jeremiah Brandreth (the 'Nottingham Captain'), William Turner, and Isaac Ludlam. The prosecution called witnesses to give evidence only of events after Oliver the spy had left Pentrich, so the lawyers for the defence were unable to show how the prisoners had been tricked into joining in the supposed plot. Failing this, there was no real excuse. They had collected weapons, they had marched as a military force, they had set out to capture Nottingham.

Fifteen witnesses were called to give evidence against Brandreth. Only one could be found for the defence. A jury of well-to-do farmers had no hesitation in declaring him guilty of High Treason. Turner and Ludlam were also found guilty and all three were sentenced to death. The others were given varying sentences of transportation.

An eyewitness at the trials compared the behaviour of the three:

'Isaac Ludlam, the elder, is a tall thin man, apparently about sixty years of age. He seems less affected by the awful situation in which he stands than William Turner was, tho' he has not that air of indifference and hardihood which Brandreth preserved throughout his trial.'

The Strutt family followed the progress of the treason trial closely. They realised that the so-called Pentrich Revolution had been caused by unemployment and hunger more than by any desire to dethrone the King or overthrow the government by force. Many other sympathetic people knew this also, but could do nothing to help the accused men. Joseph Douglas Strutt wrote to his cousin, Edward, on 9 November 1817. He began by complaining bitterly that the authorities had concealed the part taken by their own spy, Oliver, in starting the plot and encouraging the men to join it. He went on:

'I have just returned from the execution: it was a dreadful sight indeed. Many thousand people were assembled in Friar Gate, and horse soldiers were placed at Mr Hurts at the end of Ford Street. The prisoners, three of them, Brandreth, Turner and Ludlam, were brought out at 12 o'clock. Brandreth walked with a firm step on the scaffold, and looking round, said—'God be with you all and health to Lord Castlereagh.' The rope was then put round his neck, and he looked up at the beam and seemed quite composed, he certainly has a very fine countenance, his beard was not cut, and his skin looked of a fine and delicate texture.

'Turner said when he came on to the scaffold, "This is all old Oliver and the Government."

'Ludlam, who is a Methodist parson, merely addressed a prayer to the people.'

Joseph was mistaken here. It was commonly believed at the time that Ludlam, who had often led prayers and hymn singing among the prisoners, was a minister. In fact, he had been a lay preacher of a nonconformist sect.

After the hanging, the bodies of the three were beheaded, as this was still the legal punishment for high treason. A scare that troops were being sent to break up the crowd led to a hurried dispersal of the spectators. The letter concludes:

'And this is the fate of poor misguided wretches, but their blood be on their *instigators*, I say.

Goodbye, and believe me,

Your ever affectionate cousin,

J. D. Strutt.'

Hard times were not yet over for the textile workers of the Midlands or the North of England. William Felkin, the historian of the stockingers of the Midlands, remembering his youth, wrote:

'The year 1819 was a very memorable year in the history of the framework-knitters in Nottinghamshire, for the extra-ordinary severity of the sufferings of the workmen and their families. In their extremity, they frequently paraded the town, women and children heading the processions, one of which consisted of more than five thousand people. They said that by

An execution

sixteen to eighteen hours' labour they could only gain 4s to 7s a week; and that for the previous eighteen months they had not been free from the pangs of hunger.'

The town authorities became alarmed by the size of these processions and acted in the only way they could think of: 'In consequence, six companies of foot and two troops of yeomanry, with ammunition and stores, were brought into the town.'

Some of the wealthier and more compassionate citizens contributed to a special relief fund: 'Out of a fund of £3,000, three thousand families of stocking makers were relieved; and by a further sum of £4,000 subscribed for the purpose, three hundred families were enabled to emigrate to the Cape of Good Hope.' No doubt this was a generous sum and the stockingers were glad of the opportunity to begin a new life, but do you think you could hear some of the rich citizens muttering 'And good riddance'?

After 1822, with a change in the government, things began slowly to improve. The French under Napoleon had been defeated at Waterloo in 1815, and after seven years of peace and security, the governing classes in Britain were less afraid of a possible revolution. Parliament abolished the death penalty and transportation except in cases of serious crime. The use of spring-guns against poachers was declared illegal. Food became a little cheaper as the import duties were reduced. Workmen were allowed to form trade unions to try to get better wages, though they could still be punished if they overstepped the very narrow limits which the law allowed them.

As well as this, by the 1820s two generations had passed since Arkwright's first cotton mill had been built. People in the textile districts in the Midlands, in Lancashire and Yorkshire, had become accustomed to the idea of factory work, even if they did not all work in factories. They had accepted the new way of making a living and the strangeness had gone out of the machines which had seemed so threatening to the domestic workers' way of life half a century before.

6 Inventors and Machines

So far in this book you have read about some of the changes made in people's lives by the Industrial Revolution. It is now time that we saw something of the textile machines and the men who invented them.

First it is important to know how raw wool or cotton is turned into cloth. The bales or bundles of wool or cotton fibres, after being cleaned, have to be carded or combed, like combing your hair to get tangles out, so that the fibres are lying more or less parallel to each other. They are then drawn out and twisted to produce a continuous thread. This is called yarn, and the drawing out and twisting is called spinning.

Raw Cotton   Carded   Drawn Out   Twisted   Yarn

Hundreds of threads are fixed on a loom by a weaver. These are the *warp* threads. They are arranged so that all the odd threads and all the even threads can be raised alternately. When half the threads (every second one) are raised in this way, the warp looks like a roof and the shuttle can be slid across the loom, through the 'shed', that is, under the roof. The shuttle is a torpedo-shaped piece of wood which holds a bobbin. Yards and yards of thread are wound on the bobbin. This thread is called the *weft*. As the shuttle is thrown across the loom, the

73

A handloom weaver

weft trails out behind it. Then the first set of warp threads (the even ones) are lowered and the second set, the odd threads are lifted, and the shuttle carrying the weft is passed back again through the shed. The weaver goes on repeating these two actions and so a length of cloth is woven. If you examine a piece of cloth very carefully you will see that it is made up of threads woven under and over each other.

When the cloth was woven, it might be dealt with in various ways depending on what it was made of and what it was to be used for. Woollen cloth had to be brushed with teazels to fluff it up or 'raise the nap'. Any woolly bits that stuck up too much then had to be sheared or cropped, in other words, trimmed down level with the rest. This was done with huge scissors or shears. Woollen or cotton cloth could be dyed different colours. Fine cottons, calico or muslin could have patterns printed on them, using large printing blocks and coloured dyes.

Of all these processes, spinning and weaving are the most important, and in the early eighteenth century these were done by hand on fairly simple wooden machines: a spinning wheel for spinning, a hand-loom for weaving. Woollen cloth was made almost all over England, though there were three districts where it was specially important. These were in East Anglia around Norwich; in the three West of England counties of Gloucestershire, Wiltshire and Somerset; and in the West Riding of Yorkshire around Leeds and Halifax. In Lancashire, the weavers had already begun to produce a type of cloth called 'fustian' or 'cotton', for which they used wool as the warp and cotton as the weft. Cotton was also woven using linen yarn as the warp. Whatever was used as warp had to be extra strong to take the continual shuttling across and back of the shuttle carrying the weft.

During the 1750s, the Lancashire weavers began to use a gadget called the Flying Shuttle. This had been invented by a weaver named John Kay in 1733. Kay intended it to be used in weaving woollen cloth, but it did not catch on very quickly in the woollen textile districts. The Fly-Shuttle or Flying Shuttle made it possible for a weaver to pass the shuttle across his hand-loom automatically, instead of throwing it from one hand to the other. This meant he could weave twice as fast, or weave twice as much cloth in a week without giving up any of his spare time.

Domestic spinning

And when he handed the cloth over to his employer at the week-end he would get twice as much money. Now this depended on two things. First, if the employer wanted twice as much cloth. This would only be if he thought he could sell twice as much and this was why the Fly-Shuttle was not quickly accepted in the woollen industry. There was no increase in the demand for woollen cloth. There was no sense in trying to make more cloth because no one wanted to buy more. People did want cotton cloth, however, not only in England, but in other countries. Merchants could sell as much as could be made. But here came the second snag. To weave twice as much cotton cloth there would have to be twice as much cotton yarn, and the problem was how to supply it. Weavers had to spend much of their time trying to obtain enough yarn to keep them occupied. It was not unusual for a weaver to walk three or four miles in a morning and call on five or six spinners before he could collect weft to supply him for the remainder of the day.

Something was needed which would enable the spinners to spin faster—to produce a fortnight's yarn in a week. One man hit upon an idea which would help to do this. His name was James Hargreaves.

James Hargreaves was born in Oswaldtwistle, near Black-burn, in 1720, and became a handloom weaver when he grew up. He was employed by a Blackburn manufacturer to weave cloth using linen warp and cotton weft, and every weekend he would walk in to Blackburn to hand in his length of cloth and receive his pay. His wife, Elizabeth, and his daughters, Susan, Ellen, Mary and Betty did spinning and it is probable that Hargreaves in 1764 got his idea from seeing a spinning wheel accidentally knocked over:

'A number of young people were one day assembled at play in Hargreaves's house during the hour generally allotted for dinner, and the wheel at which he or some of his family were spinning, was by accident overturned. The thread still remained in the hand of the spinner, and as the arms and *periphery* of the wheel were prevented by the framing from any contact with the floor, the *velocity* it had acquired still gave motion to the spindle
76 which continued to revolve as before. Hargreaves surveyed

this with mingled curiosity and attention.'

This gave Hargreaves the idea of a machine to spin several threads at one time. He set to work and built his first Spinning Jenny, as the spinning machine came to be called. (Gin, ginny or jenny was, like 'frame' a common word at the time for any sort of mechanical device.) A writer in 1807 described the jenny:

'His first machine, which is still remembered in the neighbourhood, was made by himself, and almost wholly with a pocket knife. It contained eight spindles, and the clasp by which the thread was drawn out was the stalk of a *briar* split in two. It was a *rude* but successful attempt.'

It was in fact a multiple spinning wheel. By turning the large driving wheel, a person could spin eight threads at a time instead of one. It was the answer to the shortage of yarn, though it was not a very simple machine to operate. A modern writer who built a jenny using Hargreaves's own description and the wood and metal materials available in the 1760s, has this to say:

'The world's first successful spinning machine can hardly be said to have been the work of a mechanical genius: at one point in the winding, the operator is required to turn the driving wheel with his right hand, push forward the drawbar with his left hand and move up the *deflection wire* with his toe.'

After some practice, it was probably less difficult than it sounds, and Hargreaves's neighbours soon noticed the vast amounts of yarn which the Hargreaves's household was producing. People in the district became jealous and were afraid that if Hargreaves could spin so much yarn so quickly there would be less work and so less money for them. Some of them made threatening remarks and:

' . . . obliged him to conceal his machine, for some time after it supplied the woof or weft for his own loom. It was, however, generally known that he had made a spinning machine, and his wife, or some of his family, having boasted of having spun a pound of cotton during a short absence from the sick-bed of a neighbouring friend, the minds of the ignorant and misguided multitude became alarmed, and they shortly after broke into his house, destroyed his machine and part of his furniture.'

77

F

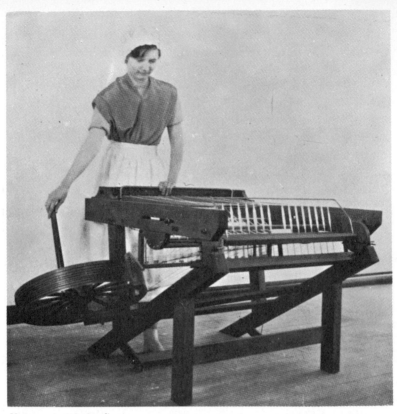

Hargreaves's Spinning Jenny

For the safety of himself and his family, James decided to move. But where? It must be somewhere that cotton yarn was in demand, but where the jenny would be safe from jealous spinners. Nottingham was the place, for the framework-knitting industry needed almost unlimited supplies of yarn, and there Hargreaves settled in the spring of 1768.

In Nottingham, he was engaged by a certain Mr Shipley to build some jennies, but he soon left him and went into partnership with Thomas James. One of James's sons described how the business was begun:

'I knew Mr Hargreaves very well; he was a stout, broad-set man, about five feet ten inches high or rather more: he first worked in Nottingham with Mr Shipley about 1768, and here my father first met with him. He was making jennies for Shipley who then wished to go into the cotton spinning. My father prevailed on him to leave Shipley and embark with him in a new concern: and money was borrowed by my father, principally on the mortgage of some freehold property, on which they were to erect their mill. The mill was erected and two dwelling houses, in one of which my father resided: in the other was Mr Hargreaves's family.'

Hargreaves obtained a patent for his jenny in 1770, but the way to build and use a jenny was already known to many other people, and Hargreaves was unable to prevent Lancashire and Nottingham cotton manufacturers from using them.

Poor Hargreaves! He not only failed to defend his jennies from rivals, but had to give up using them in his own mill because an easier way of spinning had been invented. Hargreaves and his partner realised that if they were to stay in business they would have to install the newer machines. They were already being used by their inventor, Richard Arkwright, in a mill not far from Hargreaves's own. A year later James Hargreaves died, a disappointed man.

This new machine of Richard Arkwright came to be known as the Water Frame but at first it was described as 'spinning by rollers'.

Arkwright, like Hargreaves, came from Lancashire. He was born in Preston in 1732, of poor parents. He was apprenticed to a barber and set up independently as a barber and wig-maker in Bolton in 1760. At this time, most gentlemen wore wigs and Arkwright travelled a good deal collecting hair with which to make them, from other barber shops. He must have heard a great deal of talk about the cotton trade and the difficulty of getting enough spinning done, as he waited for the barber to finish with a customer before having a word with him. Arkwright clearly saw that there was a fortune waiting for any person who could invent a spinning machine, and he made up his mind that that person would be Richard Arkwright.

He was later very guarded about how he got his ideas, but he seems to have found out all he could about such unsuccessful

Richard Arkwright

attempts at spinning machines as had already been made. In 1767, he became very friendly with a clockmaker of Warrington, named Kay, and learned from him all he could about machinery. In 1768, he returned to Preston where he persuaded a merchant, John Smalley, to provide enough money to construct a full-sized working version of his machine. Later in the year, Arkwright left Lancashire for Nottingham, having heard, as he said later, about the riots and threats against Hargreaves and the Spinning Jenny.

In Nottingham, like Hargreaves, Richard Arkwright lost no time in getting the support of wealthy partners. These were Samuel Need and Jedediah Strutt, already partners themselves in hosiery, and making good money out of the improvement to the stocking frame which Strutt had patented in 1758.

The three partners set up a 'factory' not far from Hargreaves's as we have seen. This had more claim to be called a factory because Arkwright's spinning machine was power-driven—not worked by hand like the jenny.

Arkwright's machine spun the cotton by the usual method common to the ordinary spinning wheel and the jenny—that is by holding one end of the thread and twisting it. But, as you have seen if you have tried spinning by hand, you must also keep drawing out more cotton. In the jenny, this was done by having the spindles mounted on a drawbar which was movable. Every so often, the operator pushed the drawbar to draw out more cotton to be twisted. In Arkwright's machine, the drawing out was a continuous process which was done by passing the cotton between several pairs of rollers, revolving at increasing speeds. Imagine two clothes wringers, one behind the other, the second turning faster, than the first; and a towel, say, passing through both. Do not try this, by the way, because the faster wringer, would, of course, tear the towel away from the slower one. If it were loose fibre, however, it would merely draw it out finer.

As this was a continuous process, a continuous power could be applied to the whole machine, and as Arkwright's machine was big and heavy, it could not easily be worked by hand. Some form of power, other than human muscle-power, was needed.

In his Nottingham mill, Arkwright used horse-power. A horse capstan, or horse gin, was a fairly common kind of engine in the eighteenth century. One or more horses were harnessed to a large beam, which turned horizontally on a vertical axle. The axle had a gear, or cog-wheel, on it, and from this, power could be taken by other gears or ropes and pulleys for many purposes. Horse-power was often used in this way for raising coal from pits, for drawing up water or for lifting heavy blocks of stone.

The horse-powered factory was very successful. There was a ready sale for Arkwright's yarn among the Nottinghamshire hosiers, so much so, that the jennies of Hargreaves's mill could not compete with it, as we have seen. Arkwright was also a 'pushing' businessman according to Sir Edward Baines who wrote a history of the Cotton Manufacture in 1835: 'His natural disposition was ardent, enterprising, and stubbornly persevering; his mind was as coarse as it was bold and active, and his manners were rough and unpleasing.'

He soon decided, with the approval of his partners, that roller-spinning was so successful that another factory should be started, and for this he decided to use a better form of power.

Horse-power was rather expensive. The work was so tiring that several relays of horses were used in a day and they all required stabling, feeding and care, whether they were actually working or not. What other forms of power could be used? Wind-power, of course, would be cheapest of all, and its use was well-known in windmills for grinding corn. But wind force was too variable to drive machinery which had to go at a more or less constant speed.

Water-power was clearly a better idea and it had long been known and used for grinding corn. It had, in fact, already been used, in Derby, to drive textile machinery. This was a mill for spinning silk, built by the Lombe brothers in 1717.

The patent which the Lombes held came to an end in 1732, but it was another twenty years before anyone built another silk mill. The reason was that silk was an expensive material, and not suitable for making up into the sort of everyday clothes which ordinary people want and can afford.

Arkwright, however, knew about the silk mill, with its great water-wheel, and decided that water-power was just the thing for driving his cotton spinning machines. Water-power was cheap. It was constant, unless the river froze or dried up. And it could be controlled by means of sluice gates. It was not long before Arkwright and Strutt had found a suitable site, at Cromford, and built the first water-powered cotton spinning mill to house the machines which soon came to be called water-frames.

Within six years, Arkwright and Strutt were building another mill at Cromford and one at Belper, as we have seen. Arkwright never rested. When his partnership with Strutt ended, he went into business with other men, and owned or had a share in mills at Wirksworth and Bakewell in Derbyshire, in Lancashire, and at New Lanark in Scotland. A contemporary wrote about him:

'Arkwright was a severe economist of time; and, that he might not waste a moment, he generally travelled with four horses, and at a very rapid speed.

'Arkwright commonly laboured in his *multifarious* concerns from five o'clock in the morning till nine at night; and when considerably more than fifty years of age,—feeling that the defects of his education placed him under great difficulty and inconvenience in conducting his correspondence, and in the general management of his business, he encroached upon his sleep, in order to gain an hour each day to learn English grammar, and another hour to improve his writing and *orthography*.'

It is not a surprise, then, to know that he did not consider fourteen hours too long a day for his workers!

In 1786, Arkwright was knighted by King George III and had the honour of being appointed High Sheriff of Derbyshire. He died on 3 August 1792, in the fine house he had built for himself at Cromford, the most successful of all the textile machine inventors.

The yarn which was spun on the Water Frame was rather hard and coarse. Jenny-spun yarn was fine but not very strong. To weave light yet strong cotton cloth like muslin, what was needed was yarn which would be soft, strong and fine. The man who invented a spinning machine which could do this was Samuel Crompton.

Samuel Crompton was born in 1753 and lived in a large old house called Hall-i'-th'-Wood, near Bolton, in Lancashire. He worked as a weaver and, like Hargreaves and Arkwright, he had no mechanical training. In a letter he wrote in 1802 he explained why he came to invent a spinning machine: 'About the year 1772 I Began to Endeavour to find out if possible a better Method of making Cotton Yarn than was then in General Use, being grieved at the bad yarn I had to weave.'

After five years, he perfected a spinning machine which combined the methods used by Hargreaves and Arkwright. He used it for spinning his own yarn, and neighbouring spinners

Samuel Crompton

and weavers were astonished at the fineness of the yarn and the delicacy of the cloth which was woven from it. Samuel was pestered by people wanting to see how it worked, and in the end, he accepted £106 collected among local manufacturers, to make his secret public. He never tried to patent it, but he was given an award of £5,000 by Parliament. He continued in the cotton business but was never very successful. He died in 1827.

The invention was first called the Hall-i'-th'-Wood machine, or the Muslin Wheel, but later came to be known as the Mule, because it was a 'cross' between a spinning jenny and a water-frame. It was small enough to be used in a cottage and worked by hand, but by the 1790s very much larger Mules were being used in factories and driven by water-power.

By about 1780, the spinning of cotton was almost perfect. Only minor improvements to the existing spinning machines were possible. So much yarn was being produced that it was difficult for the manufacturers to find enough people to weave it because weaving was still being done by hand.

William Radcliffe described the effect in his own district of Lancashire:

'The mule-twist now coming into *vogue*, for the warp as well as weft, added to the water-twist and common jenny yarns, with an increasing demand for every fabric the loom could produce, put all hands in request, of every age and description. The fabrics made from wool or linen vanished, while the old loom-shops being insufficient, every lumber-room, even old barns, cart-houses, and outbuildings of any description were repaired, windows broke through the old blank walls, and all fitted up for loom-shops.'

Everyone talked about the way spinning could be done faster than weaving and the problem of how to speed up weaving. An Oxford clergyman wrote this:

'Happening to be at Matlock in the summer of 1784, I fell in company with some gentlemen of Manchester, when the

Spinning mules

conversation turned on Arkwright's spinning machinery. One of the company observed, that as soon as Arkwright's patent expired, so many mills would be erected, and so much cotton spun, that hands never could be found to weave it. To this observation I replied, that Arkwright must then set his wits to work to invent a weaving mill. This brought on a conversation on the subject, in which the Manchester gentlemen unanimously agreed that the thing was impracticable; and, in defence of their opinion, they adduced arguments which I certainly was incompetent to answer, or even to comprehend, being totally ignorant of the subject, having never at that time seen a person weave.'

The name of the clergyman who had never seen anyone weaving was Edmund Cartwright. The certainty of the Manchester gentlemen that a mechanical loom was impossible nagged at his mind. He designed a machine for weaving when his holiday in Matlock was over, and hired a carpenter and a smith to construct it. He then got a weaver to set up the warp, and fill the shuttle, and a couple of men to turn the handle to make it work—if it would work. He wrote:

'To my great delight, a piece of cloth, such as it was, was the produce. As I had never before turned my thoughts to anything mechanical, either in theory or practice, nor had ever seen a loom at work, or knew anything of its construction, you will readily suppose that my first loom was a most rude piece of machinery. The warp was placed perpendicularly, the reed fell with the weight of at least half a hundredweight, and the springs which threw the shuttle were strong enough to have thrown a Congreve rocket.

Cartwright was so delighted at the time that he patented it immediately—and then went to see cloth being woven on an ordinary hand loom for the first time! He was astonished at the ease with which the weaver produced a length of cloth, and went back to make great alterations to his own invention. His final patent for the Power Loom was obtained in 1787.

It was quite a long time, however, before it was generally used. Cartwright himself put some of his looms in his own factory in Doncaster. In 1791, a Manchester firm installed Power

Power looms

Looms, and the factory was promptly burned down by angry hand-loom weavers. Other manufacturers were not then very eager to try them. Rev. Edmund Cartwright had trouble from his own looms. As they were made mainly of wood, they were constantly breaking down under the power of the steam-engine which drove them, and in the end he closed the factory down. As so few people took up the invention, Cartwright made no money out of his patent, but he was granted £10,000 by Parliament in 1801 to help pay his debts. He retired to a farm in Kent soon afterwards, and died in 1823.

Up to 1781, Arkwright's Frame and Crompton's Mule had to be driven by water power, but in that year, James Watt brought out a new version of his steam engine, which could be used to drive almost any kind of machinery. Steam power had many advantages over water power. A steam engine did consume coal which had to be bought, whereas water was free. One engine, however, could supply power for a factory which might otherwise require several water wheels. A steam engine was easily installed, compared with the weirs, cuts, and other water-works which had to be carried out for a water wheel. Steam power was more easily controlled than water power; and it was more reliable—streams did sometimes freeze over, and in periods of drought there might not be enough force of water to turn the wheel. Above all, steam power could be used in factories in towns, where coal, transport, and labour were available. Cartwright's Power Loom (although it could have been) never was used in a water-powered mill. By the time it was beginning to be used, all new factories were being built in towns, though many of the earlier ones, using water-wheels, continued to work as usual, like those in Belper.

Another change taking place in the textile industry at the same time was that iron was being used more and more instead of wood for the construction of the machines. This was partly because, as Cartwright found, wooden machines would not stand up for long to the greater force and the high-speed running which steam-power brought. It was partly so also because iron

Making wooden machinery

was now generally cheaper, and of better quality, on account of changes in the iron industry; and there were now more mechanics and engineers to maintain and repair iron machinery. Gradually, from about 1800 onwards, more and more of England's cotton was being spun and woven on iron machines, in steam-powered mills, in large towns. This new way of life brought much hardship to the workers. In Manchester, the centre of the cotton industry in the early nineteenth century, the Industrial Revolution seemed to be one of the worst things that had ever happened to people.

James Kay, a doctor, wrote a description of the way his patients lived in 1832:

'The state of the streets powerfully affects the health of the inhabitants. Sporadic cases of typhus chiefly appear in these which are narrow, ill-ventilated, unpaved, or which contain heaps of refuse, or stagnant pools.

'The houses in such situations are uncleanly, ill provided with furniture, an air of discomfort if not of squalid and loathsome wretchedness pervades them, they are often dilapidated, badly drained, damp.'

Another doctor, Peter Gaskell, describes the houses of the Manchester factory workers in greater detail, which is almost impossible to imagine:

'The houses are of the most flimsy and imperfect structure. One of the circumstances in which they are especially defective, is that of drainage and water-closets. Whole ranges of these houses are either totally undrained, or only very partially. The whole of the washings and filth from these consequently are thrown into the front or back street, which being often unpaved and cut up into deep ruts, allows them to collect into stinking and stagnant pools.'

You can see the effect of repeating the Long Rows or the Clusters of Belper over and over again without allowing any open spaces between. And of allowing two or more families to live in each house. This is what was done by builders and landlords in Manchester and other large towns:

'Many of these ranges of houses are built back to back, fronting one way into a narrow court, across which the inmates

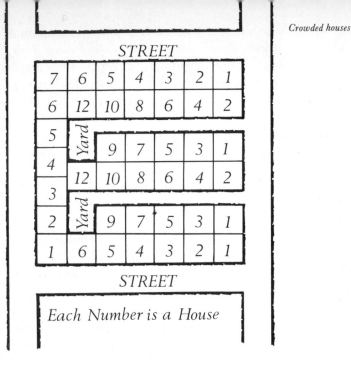

STREET

7	6	5	4	3	2	1
6	12	10	8	6	4	2
5	Yard	9	7	5	3	1
4		12	10	8	6	4	2
3	Yard					
2		9	7	5	3	1
1	6	5	4	3	2	1

STREET

Each Number is a House

of the opposite houses may shake hands without stepping out of their own doors; and the other way, into a back-street, unpaved and unsewered. Most of these houses have cellars beneath them, occupied—if it is possible to find a lower class—by a still lower class than those living above them.'

The sheer size of Manchester and other manufacturing towns also made life worse for the people living in them. It was impossible to get out of them into the country, and there were no public parks, recreation grounds or playing fields in the towns themselves.

Steam power also brought the tall smoking factory chimneys, which are still to be seen in the older parts of many industrial towns. These, pouring out smoke and soot, darkened the sky over the streets of the town, showered the washing of the more respectable housewives with smuts, blackened the stone and brickwork of shops and houses; and turned a November fog from a white woolly blanket into a choking and sometimes killing gas.

7 Gains and Losses

From the earlier chapters you will have got some idea of how the Industrial Revolution in Textiles began, and the sort of differences it made to the way people worked and the way they lived. What you have read has been almost all about cotton, because it was for the cotton industry that the new machines were invented and it was in the cotton industry that they were first used in a new system of industry—the Factory System. There are two questions to think about now: First, why did the Industrial Revolution start when it did in Britain?

To try to answer this, we can think of the growth of industry as you might think of the growth of a plant. You know that a seedling must have the right conditions or it will not grow, that is, it must be planted in good soil, it must have a certain warmth, it must be kept moist and it must have light and air.

What are the conditions in which an industry will grow? What are the things which an industry needs? First, the raw materials to make the goods. Then, people with the knowledge and skill to do the work. And lastly, enough people willing to buy the goods which are made.

Now, in Britain in the second half of the eighteenth century, all three conditions were present. There was wool, and a large merchant navy to bring in endless supplies of cotton. There was plenty of coal for the steam engines, when steam power was applied in factories, and plenty of iron ore, with which to make the machines.

There was also the skill, which could be put to use in the textile industry. Millwrights who were used to building for corn mills could do the same for water-powered spinning mills.

Wood-turners and carpenters who were used to making furniture did not find it too difficult to build the first wooden machines. It was easy for a clock-maker to understand and make the more intricate parts of the spinning machines. People who had spun on an ordinary spinning wheel could easily understand how a jenny or a water-frame worked. A man who could use a stocking-frame would have the skill to learn how to work any of the textile machines invented in the eighteenth century.

But no one will invent machines and build a factory to house them unless he believes that he can sell the things which his factory is making. There must be a demand for the goods, that is, enough people willing to buy them. This also happened in England in the second half of the eighteenth century. The population began to increase, from about five and a half million people in 1750 to about nine million in 1800. This meant nearly twice as many people to buy goods, and certainly very willing to buy them. A writer in 1785 stated:

'Now cotton yarn is cheaper than linen yarn; and cotton goods are very much used in place of cambrics, lawns and other expensive fabrics of flax; and they have almost totally superseded the silks. Women of all ranks, from the highest to the lowest, are clothed in British manufactures of cotton, from the muslin cap on the crown of the head, to the cotton stocking under the sole of the foot.

'With the gentlemen, cotton stuffs for waiscoats have almost superceded woollen cloths; and they have the advantage, like the ladies' gowns, of having a new and fresh appearance every time they are washed. Cotton stockings have also become very general for summer wear.'

And as Britain was already trading with the rest of the world, there were many millions more in foreign countries who were keen to buy cloth and other things made by machine in Britain rather than pay more for things made by hand in their own country.

There was something else as well which helped the Industrial Revolution to start in Britain during the eighteenth century. That was money.

Most manufacturers like Jedediah Strutt were not very

Ladies' clothes in fine cotton

wealthy to start with and had to borrow money to build their mills. Luckily, there were many people in Britain in the eighteenth century who were rich and thrifty enough to have money to lend. Trading companies had been making good profits since the seventeenth century, and merchants who had made money by trading with the East, or the West, Indies, or the American Colonies, were willing to invest money in industry. Professional men, like doctors and lawyers, also lent money to men setting up in manufacture, contributed to turnpike trusts and bought shares in canal companies. What was very important was that the people who had a few hundred

G

pounds to lend were willing to put it to use instead of hoarding it away. They were confident that in industry it would be safe and that their share of the profits of manufacture would be large.

The second question we must try to answer is about factories. Why did the factory system start in the cotton industry?

One main reason was that if machines were to be used, they could not be driven by water-power or steam-power at the workers' own homes. There were other reasons, however, which made the idea of a mill or a factory attractive to employers. You will remember that when Hargreaves moved to Nottingham, he built a mill to house his jennies. Now, the jenny was a fairly small machine, and was worked by hand. Why then, did Hargreaves have a mill which was merely a building large enough to hold about fifty jennies? Why did he and his partner not employ people to spin with jennies in their own homes, as the hosiers employed the stockingers? One reason was that the jennies would be safer in a mill in case anyone should want to smash them up. It was also much easier for the employer to insist on higher standards of workmanship if he could supervise the work on his own premises.

A third reason for housing hand-powered jennies in a mill was to prevent rival spinners from seeing one and constructing their own. Even if an inventor got a patent for his machines, he himself had to find out and prosecute anyone pirating his invention.

It was, therefore, an advantage to the employer to have his workers all in one building and under his supervision while they worked (like pupils working in class compared with pupils doing homework). The big power-driven machines, however, made factories not only desirable but essential.

Factories were well-liked by the employers, but what of the workers, and what of the general public who were neither factory owners nor 'hands'? Some people thought and wrote of a Golden Age before the Industrial Revolution, believing that people had been better off before there were any factories.

Dr Gaskell, whose account of the Manchester slums you have

read in Chapter 6, had this to say about the existence of the working classes before the 1760s:

'These were, undoubtedly, the golden times of manufactures, considered in reference to the character of the labourers. By all the processes being carried on under a man's own roof, he retained his individual respectability; he was kept apart from associations which might injure his moral worth, whilst he generally earned wages which were sufficient not only to live comfortably upon, but which enabled him to rent a few acres of land; thus joining in his own person two classes, that are now daily becoming more and more distinct.'

Although Gaskell wrote as if he knew all about the golden times before the 1760s, it is worth noticing that he himself was not born till 1806. He was very anxious that something should be done to improve the housing and health of the poor in places like Manchester. Perhaps he felt that by making a clear contrast between conditions in 1833 and earlier conditions, he could make his readers more sympathetic towards the poor.

Some of the things he approved of in the working man, under the domestic system would not, perhaps, appeal to us at the present day. The worker had

'. . . an utter ignorance of printed books, beyond the thumbed Bible and a few theological tracts; seeking his stimulus in home-brewed ale; having for his support animal food occasionally, but living generally upon farm produce, meal or rye bread, eggs, cheese, milk, butter, etc; the use of tea quite unknown, or only just beginning to make its appearance; a sluggish mind in an active body.'

Do you think that books and tea would have a bad effect on the working-class? And how many people would like to be held up as an example of 'a sluggish mind in an active body'?

Richard Guest, writing in 1823, noted the dullness of the working-class before the Industrial Revolution:

'The greatest varieties of scene which they witnessed were the market day of the village, and the attendance at church on the Sabbath; and the *summum bonum* of their lives was to sit vacant and inactive in each others' houses, to sun themselves in the market place, or talk over news at that great mart of village gossip, the blacksmith's shop.'

A political discussion

And he mentioned the mental changes brought about by the growth of the cotton manufacture:

'The operative workmen being thrown together in great numbers, and their *faculties* sharpened and improved by constant communication. Conversation wandered over a variety of topics not before *essayed*: the questions of Peace and War, which interested them importantly, inasmuch as they might produce a rise or fall of wages, became highly interesting, and this brought them into the vast field of politics and discussions on the character of their Government, and the men who composed it.'

Gaskell and Guest agreed that before the growth of industrial towns, the average workman was mentally dull, but Gaskell notes it with approval while Guest treats it rather with scorn. Yet Dr Kay was of a different opinion:

'Prolonged and exhausting labour, continued from day to day, and from year to year, is not calculated to develop the intellectual or moral faculties of man. The mind gathers neither stores nor strength from the constant extension and retraction of the same muscles. The intellect slumbers in *supine inertness*.'

Another writer in the early nineteenth century, however, was convinced that factory work had no ill effects either on the body or the mind:

'Factory labour is far less injurious than many of the most common and necessary employments of civilised life. It is much less irksome than that of the weaver, less arduous than that of the smith, less *prejudicial* to the lungs, the spine, and the limbs, than those of the shoemaker and the tailor.

'On visiting mills, I have generally remarked the coolness and *equanimity* of the workpeople, even of the children, whose manner seldom, as far as my observation goes, indicates anxious care, and is more frequently sportive than gloomy.'

One man, who had a reply to that remark, was John Fielden, who began work in his father's mill at the age of ten. When he grew up, he became an M.P. and worked hard to have the hours of work reduced by law. In 1836, he wrote a book called 'The Curse of the Factory System' in which he described his own feelings:

'For several years after I began to work in the mill, the hours of labour at our works did not exceed ten in the day, winter and summer; and even with the labour of those hours, I shall never forget the fatigue I often felt before the day ended, and the anxiety of us all to be relieved from the unvarying and irksome toil we had gone through before we could obtain relief by such play and amusement as we resorted to when liberated from our work. I allude to this fact, because it is not uncommon for persons to infer, that, because the children who work in factories are seen to play like other children, when they have time to do so, the labour is, therefore, light, and does not fatigue them.'

Some people at the time, and many people at the present, picture textile mills as dark gloomy places, and millowners as harsh and brutal employers. Perhaps they think of the phrase of Blake's—'those dark Satanic mills'—and if the mills were so, who should we expect the employer to be? A man like Ellis Needham whom you met in Chapter Three would fit the description. You might think that at best the workers would regard their employer as someone who paid them rather grudgingly for their long hours of work. A person to fear, to grumble about in private conversations, to show a sullen respect to when he appeared? In many cases, certainly this was so, but there were some who were regarded as heroes by their workers. Richard Arkwright was one of these.

In October 1778, the 'Derby Mercury' printed the following: The occasion was a procession, and a feast given by Arkwright, and the song, 'composed on the Occasion by one of the Workmen, was sung in full Chorus, amongst Thousands of Spectators from Matlock Bath, and the neighbouring Towns, who testified their Satisfaction at so pleasing a Sight'.

SONG

Tune—Roast Beef of Old England

Ye num'rous Assembly that make up this Throng
Spare your Mirth for a Moment and list to my Song,
The Bounties let's sing, that our Master belong,
　At the Cotton-Mills now at Cromford,
　The famous renown'd Cotton-Mills.

You know he provides us a Feast once a Year,
With Fruit, Cakes, and Liquor, our Spirits to cheer,
He asks no Return, but we decent appear, &c.

Ye Hungry and Naked all hither repair,
No longer in Want don't remain in Despair,
You'll meet with Employment, and each gets a Share, &c.

Ye Crafts and Mechanics, if ye will draw nigh,
No longer ye need to lack an Employ,
And each duly paid, which is a great Joy, &c.

To our noble Master, a Bumper then fill,
The matchless Inventor of this Cotton-Mill,
Each toss off his Glass with a hearty Good-will,
　With Huzza for the Mills now at Cromford,
　All join with a jovial Huzza.

The people who roared this out in Cromford were clearly in no doubt that they were better-off for being Mr Arkwright's mill-hands. What did John Byng, the aristocratic traveller, think about what he saw? His diary tells us. The entry is 18 June 1790:

'By two o'clock I was at the Black Dog at Cromford; around which is much levelling of ground, and increase of buildings. This house, and village appear so clean, and so gay, as quite to revive me, after the dirt and dullness of Bakewell.

'I dare not, perhaps I shou'd not, *repine* at the increase of our trade, and (partial) population; yet speaking as a tourist, these vales have lost all their beauties; the rural cot has given place to the lofty red mill, and the grand houses of overseers; the stream perverted from its course by sluices, and aqueducts, will no longer ripple and cascade. Every rural sound is sunk in the clamours of cotton works; and the simple peasant is changed into the impudent mechanic—the woods find their way into the canals; and the rocks are disfigured for limestone.'

The simple peasant living in his rural cot—this was an idea which appealed to many people who wished that the Industrial Revolution had never begun. Gaskell also wrote with admiration of 'the same generation living age after age on the same spot, and under the same thatched roof, which thus became a sort of heir-loom endeared to its occupier by a long series of happy memories and home delights.'

This may have been true in many cases, but it is hard to see why Gaskell could be so sure that the memories associated with a thatched cottage should always have been happy ones. Let us see what another visitor to Cromford wrote about rural cottages before the mills were built:

'Another mill, as large as the first, is building here; new houses are rising round it; and everything wears the face of industry and cheerfulness: how different this from the description given some years ago, when this place was described as "the habitation of a few grovers who dug for lead-ore, and whose huts were not bigger than hogsties".'

Perhaps by now you are feeling rather confused, and saying that for every person who thought things were better and people better-off under the Domestic System there were as many who said that they were better under the Factory System. Perhaps you may be thinking that a lot depended on the sort of person who was writing about textile factories; that one person could see good points which another person might not notice. We do not think of cotton mills as beautiful buildings and yet John Byng, who saw them mainly as destroying the country scenery of the Derwent Valley, could also write: 'These cotton mills, seven stories high, and filled with inhabitants, remind me of a first rate man-of-war; and when they are lighted up, on a dark night, look most luminously beautiful.'

A lady, writing about another Derbyshire mill, said, even more poetically: 'When darkness pervades the Dale, and the innumerable large windows are lighted up, not even the out-line of the building to be traced against the dark mountain, it might be thought to be an illuminated palace raised by the power of magic.'

Can we not say, then, that people in general gained any benefits from the Industrial Revolution? Or did they lose more than they gained? We cannot answer simply yes or no. You can try to draw up a sort of balance sheet of gains and losses, if you like, and see if you can come to any conclusion. One thing is true, at any rate. People living at the time found out the evils, and tried to cure these without at the same time remov-ing the benefits.

The employment of children in mills was the first thing which seemed obviously wrong, and in 1802 Parliament passed the first Factory Act, limiting hours of work and laying down rules for the treatment of the so-called apprentices. But the inspection of factories was left to the J.P.s and most of them took little trouble over it. In 1816 Richard Arkwright (the son of the inventor) told members of the House of Commons: 'That Act has not been followed up, with respect to the visiting of magistrates, for these thirteen years. I think they visited my mills at Cromford twice.'

In 1819 another Act was passed, which this time applied to any children working in cotton mills only, although the idea of factories was already spreading from the cotton to the woollen industry.

In 1830 a great campaign was started in Yorkshire to urge M.P.s to pass yet another and more effective Act. The leaders of the campaign pointed out that although Britain was preparing to abolish Negro slavery in the West Indian plantations, nothing was being done about the child 'slaves' in factories in Britain itself. Parliament decided to appoint certain Members to find out the facts, and a great verbal battle began between those who wanted to improve conditions for child factory workers and those who wanted no interference by the State in factories. Those who were against child labour were easily able to find examples of over-work, cruelty, and deformity. The M.P.s heard Samuel Coulson describe in answer to questioning, how he and his wife got their children off to work: 'In the early time we had to take them up asleep and shake them, when we could get them on the floor to dress them, before we could get them off to work; but not so in the common hours.'

The common hours of work in this mill were 6 a.m. to 8-30 p.m. The early time or brisk time lasted for about six weeks at a stretch and the hours were 3 a.m. to 10 p.m.:

'Supposing they had been a little too late, what would have been the consequence during the long hours?'

'They were quartered in the longest hours, the same as in the shortest time.'

'What do you mean by quartering?'

'A quarter was taken off.'

'If they had been how much too late?'

'Five minutes.'

'What was the length of time they could be in bed during those long hours?'

'It was near 11 o'clock before we could get them into bed after getting a little victuals, and then at morning my mistress used to stop up all night, for fear that we could not get them ready for the time.'

Elizabeth Bentley gave evidence herself. She was twenty-three and worked in a flax mill in Leeds:

'What time did you begin to work in a factory?'

'When I was six years old.'

'What were your hours of labour in that mill?'

'From five in the morning till nine at night, when they were *thronged*.'

A cartoon to raise sympathy

'You are considerably deformed in your person in consequence of this labour?'

'Yes, I am.'

'You were perfectly straight and healthy before you worked at a mill?'

'Yes, I was as straight a little girl as ever went up and down town.'

Doctors and surgeons gave their opinions of the effects on health of working long hours, and mill-owners were found who did not employ children younger than ten, and worked only twelve hours a day, including an hour or more for meals.

At last, in 1833, the first really effective Factory Act was passed—effective because the government appointed four Inspectors to see that the rules were being kept. No children under nine were to work in textile mills. The maximum hours of work for children between nine and thirteen were nine hours a day or forty-eight hours in a week. For young persons between thirteen and eighteen, the maximum hours were twelve hours a day or sixty-nine hours per week. No one under eighteen was to work at night, and children under thirteen must have two hours' schooling a day.

You will see by comparing this with the conditions mentioned in Chapter 3 that what Parliament laid down in 1833 was no more than what had been the usual custom of good factory owners for fifty years or more. Now all mill-owners would have to keep these terms, or be fined for breaking the law.

One thing we can say about the employment of children in textile mills: it seems to have got upper and middle class people interested in the whole subject of child labour. The Act of 1833 was the beginning of a whole succession of laws which made things easier for children working; not only in textile factories but in mines, brick-yards and other places where conditions were sometimes even worse than in the worst mills.

The majority of people agreed that children needed to be protected by law from mean or harsh employers. Adult workers were considered to be able to fend for themselves. To do this, men felt that they should band together, or form a combination, as the phrase was. The combining of workmen to hold out for higher wages or better working conditions was made illegal by the Combination Acts of 1799 and 1800. In 1824, however, the Combination Acts were abolished, and it became safer for workmen to form Trade Unions, which could bargain with employers for shorter hours or better pay.

Another way in which some of the evils of the Industrial Revolution began slowly to be overcome was by Friendly Societies among the people themselves. Each member paid a few pence weekly into the Society fund. When a large sum of money was needed, usually in cases of illness or death, the member could draw out an agreed amount. These Friendly Societies were often connected with a religious group. In the 1830s, Belper had a Church Sunday School Sick and Funeral Society, a Wesleyan Society, and a Total Abstinence Sick and Funeral Society. These usually met in a schoolroom or a chapel, but there were others which met in some of the inns of the town and usually spent some of their funds on the premises.

By the 1830s then, some of the hardships connected with the Industrial Revolution had begun to be cured; child labour by 103

Manchester Mills

the action of Parliament, adults' wages by Trade Union bargaining, the lack of a reserve of money by the Friendly Societies among the workers themselves.

By the 1830s the textile industries were growing strongly. The factory system was well established—a cotton mill was no longer a curiosity that a traveller would go out of his way to see. But we cannot say that the Industrial Revolution was over. It was just that the novelty had worn off. People were beginning to take inventions as something to be expected. In a sense, the Industrial Revolution is still going on, with still newer types of materials—plastics, new ways of producing power to drive machines—atomic energy, new methods of transporting goods—hovercraft. Can you make a list of the continuing changes in industry in the past twenty, forty, sixty years? And what about twenty, forty, or sixty years ahead, into the future? Are people happier now than sixty years ago, or one hundred and sixty years ago? And what will you think about it in sixty years' time?

Where Does All the Information Come from?

If you want to find out how people's ways of making a living changed in your own town or village, it is best to start by finding books on local history by modern writers. Most of the larger Public Libraries have a section on local history. There should also be printed books of the 1700s and 1800s often written by tourists or travellers who described each district they visited. Old newspapers give accounts of events and contain advertisements which are often very interesting. There may be some maps in your local library also, showing your county or district at different times in the past.

Your county Record Office may have material which is not printed—court records, account books, collections of letters, and so on. There may also be old letters, diaries and business accounts in private hands which give valuable information about local firms and the sort of jobs people had.

Parliamentary records include details of Acts authorising the building of canals, turnpike roads and railways, as well as Factory Acts, and reports of commissions on child labour, conditions in towns, etc.

Some information can only be obtained by going to where factories and works stood and seeing what still remains of the earlier buildings. The study and recording by photographs, drawings, and plans, of mills, canals, and machinery of past times really began on a large scale only in the 1950s. It is called Industrial Archaeology. There is a series of books on Industrial Archaeology dealing with each region of Britain which will tell you about some of the things to see in your own area, but there are many buildings and other things which may never have been recorded in any book. Your local history society would be able to supply information about some of these, and would be very pleased if you were to discover something which they did not already know about.

Things to Do

1 Find out the population of your town or village about 1700, 1800, 1850, 1900, and at present. Has it increased? If so, try to discover when the increase started and why.

2 What are the main industries in your town or district? Can you find out how long ago they were started, and why?

3 Write a letter dated 1740, asking the parish overseer to pay you some poor relief. Explain your family's circumstances.

4 Illustrate some scenes from the apprenticeship of Robert Blincoe.

5 Write a letter as someone in 1776 who has just started work in Strutt's mill, urging a friend to do the same.

6 Illustrate some scenes from the Rejoicings in 1814.

7 You are a grocer, married, with three children aged between six and twelve. You are thinking of setting up in business in Belper in 1820. Make a list of the points in favour.

8 Write and make a speech as a Luddite leader urging men to join in an attack on a mill.

9 Imagine you are one of Captain Phillipp's Hussars. Describe how you captured the 'rebels' in 1817.

10 Imagine you are a lawyer for the men in the Pentrich Revolution. Write and make a speech asking the jury to acquit them.

11 Find out all you can about Acts after 1833, which limited children's work in textile mills and other places.

12 Write and make a speech as an M.P. asking the House of Commons to pass a law to make things easier for children in factories.

13 Have a class debate on whether the Industrial Revolution did more harm than good.

Glossary

This is a list of special words. If the word you want to know is not here, look for it in your dictionary.

affluence, wealth
appositely, suitably
briar, wild rose bush
cavalcade, procession of people on horseback
chastisement, correction; punishment
civility, politeness; civilised behaviour
commendation, praise
concourse, crowd
concur, agree
deflection wire, a wire which moves the threads from the spinning to the
   winding position
delusion, mistaken idea
deposition, statement
devoirs, duty; here the phrase means they had drunk enough
dimensions, measurements
Dissenters, Protestants who do not belong to the Church of England
divers, various
embezzling, taking something for yourself which another person has
   given you to use
equanimity, contentment
equipage, carriage
essayed, tried out
exceeds, is more than
faculties, intelligence
furmenty, fine porridge
guising, dressing up to act a part
imprecations, curses
inconsiderable, unimportant
indenture, a written legal agreement; a contract
indicted, accused
insignificant, unimportant
instigators, those who put ideas into other people's heads
instrumentality, action
insurgents, rebels

insurrection, rebellion
invoice, a list of goods which are being sent
javelin men, armed bodyguard of a sheriff
meritorious, excellent
multifarious, many different
mumming, mimeing; acting without speaking
officiate, take the leading part
orthography, spelling
periphery, outer edge
pike, a sharp iron spike on a long handle
plaudits, applause
prejudicial, dangerous
premium, bonus; extra pay
prodigious, most unusual
Providence, God; good fortune
purloining, stealing
putrid, rotten
repine, complain
repulsed, beaten back
respited, postponed
retinue, column
rude, rough
sedition, revolt
se'nnight, a week ago
spole, spool; a reel on which thread is wound
summum bonum, greatest joy
supine inertness, idle dullness
tenantry, tenants
tender, an offer to do a job for a certain price
thronged, busy with work
toll, a tax paid by all users of certain roads
toll-house, a house beside a toll gate in which the keeper lived
Unitarians, members of the Unitarian Church; a certain group of

utility, usefulness
vehement, violent
velocity, speed
vogue, fashion
warp, the threads which run the length of a piece of cloth
weft, the threads which go across a piece of cloth
wrought, brought about
yeomanry, wealthy farmers

1780 Milford Mill built.

1781 Watt patents his second steam engine.

1782 Watt engine introduced at Masborough works.

1783 *Treaty of Versailles.*

1784 Cort patents the Puddling and Rolling process. Mail coaches started.

1785 Cartwright invents the Power Loom. Steam powered cotton mill at Papplewick, Notts.

1786 Second Belper Mill.   First Mill School in Belper.

1787

1788

1789 *French Revolution.*

1790 Elsecar new pit sunk.

1791

1792 Milford Warehouse. Third Belper Mill started. Cromford Canal built. Postal service

1793 Dearne and Dove Canal built. *War of French Revolution begins.*   in Belper.

1794 *Habeas Corpus Act suspended.* Newton Chambers opened Chapeltown works.

1795 Speenhamland System of Poor Relief started.

1796 First rolling mill at Wortley ironworks. Barnsley canal built.

1797

1798

1799 First Combination Act.

1800 Second Combination Act. *Act of Union with Ireland.*

1801 General Enclosure Act.

1802 Factory Apprentices Act. *Peace of Amiens.*

1803 North Mill, Belper burnt down.

1804 Trevithick builds his railway locomotive.

1805 *Napoleonic War begins. Battle of Trafalgar.*

1806

1807 *Slave Trade abolished.*

1808

1809

1810 Riots in Sheffield.

1811 Luddite Riots in Nottingham.

1812 Luddite Riots.

1813

1814

1815 Miners' Safety Lamp invented. Corn Law passed. *Battle of Waterloo.*

1816 *Peterloo. The Six Acts.* Pentrich 'Revolution'.

1817

1818

1819 Factory Act.